Date Due

POETRY: DIRECT AND OBLIQUE

POETRY
DIRECT AND OBLIQUE

By

E. M. W. TILLYARD

LITT.D., F.B.A.
MASTER OF JESUS COLLEGE
CAMBRIDGE

BARNES & NOBLE, Inc., New York
Publishers • Booksellers • Since 1873

PUBLISHED BY
Chatto & Windus Ltd
LONDON

*

Oxford University Press
TORONTO

51489

FIRST PUBLISHED 1934
REVISED AND RESET 1945
REPRINTED 1948
REPRINTED 1956
REPRINTED 1959

PRINTED IN GREAT BRITAIN

PREFACE

POETRY DIRECT AND OBLIQUE was published in 1934. In 1940 the remaining stock of copies was destroyed by enemy action. This accident had the advantage of allowing me to recast what I had come to see was too prolix a book. I have simplified the arrangement, cut down the bulk severely, and substituted or added a little new matter. I hope that the present version is more lucid and readable. In one sense it is not a new book, for this is not quite how I should expound my theme if I did so now for the first time. But it should be a new book in the sense that it makes a different impression from its original version; and I should be glad if it could be considered such.

In the first version the emphasis fell equally on critical theory and on the criticism of texts. Now, the criticism of texts comes first, and the critical theory exists largely in order to promote it. In fact my chief aim is to suggest to the common reader ways of looking at poetry that may help him to get further into the meaning of some of the poems he has read or will read, and hence to enjoy them better.

I have taken some of my examples from classical literature; and it might be objected that this is not the way to please the common reader. I can at least plead that nearly all the classical references are to the best-known works of the best-known authors. And anyhow the classical examples are not a big proportion of the whole.

E. M. W. T.

CONTENTS

Chapter I
INTRODUCTORY

Chapter II
STATEMENT

Chapter III
OBLIQUITY

8

Chapter 1

INTRODUCTORY

1. PRELIMINARY

JOHNSON in attacking *Lycidas* provided a classic example of criticism that errs through a false assumption. *Lycidas* is an elegy; an elegy professes to lament the death of a revered or beloved person; and Johnson assumes that an elegy should be judged by the standards it professes. He found that *Lycidas* did not fulfil its professions:

> It is not to be considered as the effusion of real passion; for passion runs not after remote allusions and obscure opinions. . . . Where there is leisure for fiction, there is little grief.

Johnson assumed that *Lycidas* is what I shall call 'direct' poetry or the poetry of 'statement,' and by such a standard he found it wanting. Actually the poem is far other than what it professes to be. Its main concern embraces vastly more than grief at the death of Edward King. It expresses a personal mental experience and a general moral truth. And it does so not by direct statement but obliquely by implication. This distinction between 'direct' and 'oblique' poetry will be elaborated in the next section. It suffices here to say that Johnson's attack is invalidated from the start because he has put the poem in the wrong category.

Critics to-day are not likely to make Johnson's specific error, but they are not always clear in their minds what degree of directness or obliquity they assume the poems they are judging to possess. They run the risk of going astray initially, just as Johnson did. And the danger of being deceived to-day by a specious obliquity may not be less than the converse one of being deceived by a specious directness. The distinction between 'direct' and 'oblique' poetry is not new, and must be familiar enough in some form or another, but as an important initial criterion I doubt if it has been clearly formulated or consciously applied to critical practice. This book suggests a scale ranging from the greatest possible directness to the greatest possible obliquity in poetry. Between the two extremes the gradations are of course innumerable; and the scale is only of the roughest. But still it should help to eliminate the mistake of judging poems by standards to which they have no reference.

But when you have fixed your poem in the scale, you have not begun seriously to criticise it. All you have done is to put it in a position where you can see it without a certain preliminary distortion. Now if you conclude that a poem is oblique, you are not likely to get very far with it until you discover what it is that has been given oblique expression. In writing a book on Milton I was confronted with this problem when I came to *Lycidas*, and flattered myself that I had got a little way behind that poem's façade. At any rate, I was attempting a kind of criticism of which there is too little and whose possibilities are large. One object of this book is to exploit this kind of criticism through a series of practical demonstrations.

The relations of direct and oblique poetry have their bearing on the general poetic health of a given epoch; including that of our own day; and I have inserted some historical comment, and drawn contemporary morals.

The terms 'direct' and 'oblique' poetry are a false contrast. All poetry is more or less oblique: there is no direct poetry. But the terms 'less oblique' and 'more oblique' would sound ridiculous; and the only way to be emphatic or even generally intelligible is by exaggeration to force a hypothetical but convenient contrast.

I use the words *direct, oblique, statement,* etc., in ways that are convenient rather than quite consistent. I make *direct statement,* or merely *statement,* or *directness,* stand for the same notion; as I make *oblique statement,* or *obliquity,* stand for the opposed notion.

2. THE TWO VILLAGE-GREENS

A familiar contrast, directed usually to illustrating some differences between Augustan and Romantic styles of poetry, is that between Goldsmith's picture of Auburn in *The Deserted Village* and Blake's *Echoing Green* in *Songs of Innocence*. And these two pieces will serve neatly enough as text for the quite different contrast I have to explain. Here is Goldsmith's village-green with the pleasures that enlivened it:

> How often have I loitered o'er thy green,
> Where humble happiness endeared each scene!
> How often have I paused on every charm,
> The sheltered cot, the cultivated farm,
> The never-failing brook, the busy mill,
> The decent church that topt the neighbouring hill,
> The hawthorn bush, with seats beneath the shade,
> For talking age and whispering lovers made!
> How often have I blest the coming day,
> When toil remitting lent its turn to play,
> And all the village train from labour free
> Led up their sports beneath the spreading tree,
> While many a pastime circled in the shade,
> The young contending as the old surveyed;
> And many a gambol frolicked o'er the ground,
> And slights of art and feats of strength went round;
> And still as each repeated pleasure tired,
> Succeeding sports the mirthful band inspired.

This is a fair example of the poetry of direct statement: it is to some degree concerned with what the words state as well as with what they imply. Had Goldsmith been describing one actual village, were it certain that he were describing an actual remembered scene at Lissoy, the element of statement would be solider than it is; and in that he is imagining his village on the analogy of a number of villages he has known, he is the less direct. But at least he wants the reader to think primarily of villages when he talks of Auburn; not of the Social Contract or of heavenly beatitude. We believe this because the formal parts of the poetry reinforce the statement rather than suggest thoughts alien to it. The couplets evolve in a simple explicatory sequence; they unfold the scene with no hint of ulterior meaning; their freshness and unobstructedness are those of the clear sunny day they describe. The vocabulary is as close to simple statement as Goldsmith's epoch allowed to anyone but a rebel; and when he is not simple, it is for convention's sake and not with any view to obliquity. Thus by 'humble happiness' he probably means 'humble, happy people,' and by 'talking age' he certainly means 'garrulous old folk': but these phrases are no more than the poetic idiom of his day.

True, some obliquity cannot be denied. Goldsmith wants to say that he likes villagers to be hard-working and sober and to enjoy simple pleasures, and in that he says so, not by a general statement but through describing an imagined single occasion when the villagers enjoy these pleasures, he is being slightly oblique. And there is another, much more important example of obliquity. Goldsmith idealises his Auburn not only because this is how he would like villages to be, but because, feeling homesick for some place other than the one he is in, he must imagine his perfect refuge. Thus, when he says,

> And still as each repeated pleasure tired,
> Succeeding sports the mirthful band inspired,

he reveals himself day-dreaming of perpetually unexhausted pleasure, forgetful of the cruel actual law of diminishing returns.

For all this, Goldsmith's lines mainly concern their professed subject, village-life, and therefore exemplify the poetry of statement.

Here is Blake's village-green:

> The Sun does arise,
> And make happy the skies;

The merry bells ring
To welcome the Spring;
The skylark and thrush,
The birds of the bush,
Sing louder around
To the bells' chearful sound,
While our sports shall be seen
On the Echoing Green.

Old John, with white hair,
Does laugh away care,
Sitting under the oak,
Among the old folk.
They laugh at our play,
And soon they all say:
'Such, such were the joys
When we all, girls and boys,
In our youth time were seen
On the Echoing Green.'

Till the little ones, weary,
No more can be merry;
The sun does descend,
And our sports have an end.
Round the laps of their mothers
Many sisters and brothers,
Like birds in their nest,
Are ready for rest,
And sport no more seen
On the darkening Green.

It is very easy to allow to Blake's lines just about the same amount of directness and obliquity as to Goldsmith's. Blake's is the greater mind, and of course he uses a different language; but he has every appearance of describing as real a village as Goldsmith's and of knowing quite as much about village games. The sunshine has got into Blake's verse no less than into Goldsmith's. Blake, too, is using his village to express approval of a way of life. He finds in the traditional village sports and pieties a type of his world of innocence, a wider notion perhaps than Goldsmith's more didactic approval. All this is true as far as it goes, and did it respond to our feelings about *The Echoing Green* we might be content with criticising the poem by standards of no profounder obliquity than satisfied *The Deserted Village*.

Now the statements that confront us in *The Echoing Green* have so solid an appearance, present so winningly confident a front, that it seems initially ridiculous not to take them as the poem's major concern. It is the structure that should first put us on our guard. Blake's three verses contrast emphatically with the leisurely roll-out of Goldsmith's couplets. Dawn in the first stanza. Why in the second does Old John sit under the oak? To keep off the noonday sun. Evening in the third. The form is a stylised day-cycle; and if we heed this form, some element of abstraction is set up against the concrete activities of the villagers. There is a careful balance of idea between opening and close: the echoing green becomes the darkening green to balance (though not for this reason only) the rising sun of the first line; the awakening birds in the first stanza are balanced by the simile 'like birds in their nest' in the last. Congruently with the full noonday heat and light the old unfreeze and join their mirth to make up a full chorus with the children. Why all this ingenuity? Does it merely add a pleasing regularity to the statement, or is it a symptom of something else? The truth is that Blake is expressing an idea, an idea that has nothing in itself to do with birds, old and young folk, or village-greens, and one of those most common in Blake's poetical works. It is the idea that there is a virtue in desire satisfied. Though desire is not mentioned, yet the keynote of the poem is fruition. Nature fulfils itself in the cycle of a perfect day. Old John gets a perfect vicarious satisfaction, the little ones are utterly played out and ready for rest. And at the end the 'echoing green' is the 'darkening green' because its function is fulfilled. The very completeness of formal balance points the same way. The poem gives the sense of the perfectly grown apple that comes off at a touch of the hand. It expresses the profound peace of utterly gratified desire.

Thus explained, *The Echoing Green* is as nearly perfect an example of poetical obliquity as can be found. The main sense is stated in no particular whatever, but is diffused through every part of the poem and can be apprehended as a whole only through the synthesis of all those parts. The abstract idea, far from being stated, has been translated into completely concrete form; it has disappeared into apparently alien facts. Through its major obliquity *The Echoing Green* is in a different category from Goldsmith's lines and must be judged by different standards.

Even if this interpretation of *The Echoing Green* be wrong (and such bold guesses at obliquity are likely to please oneself better than others), the *principle* illustrated is not thereby invalidated. Those who reject this instance may find a better and agree that directness and obliquity must vary widely from poem to poem and that to judge an oblique poem as if it were direct, and the other way round, can only lead to disaster.

Chapter II

STATEMENT

I. THE SPHERE OF STATEMENT

IT is a mistake to suppose that because statement is nearer to prose than obliquity it belongs to the world's less primitive and more sophisticated ages. On the contrary, direct poetry can spring from a deep part of our nature. One of the uses of art is to order our experiences by re-enacting them; and such re-enactment is a primitive habit. Historians of the ballad tell us that the fishermen of the Faroe Islands mimed, after they had landed home, any especially exciting adventure in their voyage. J. H. Driberg found that the African tribes whose habits he studied used poetry as a matter of course to recount and thus to re-enact even the ordinary happenings of their lives. And Aristotle's notion that poetry springs from the instinct of imitation must surely include this idea; just as his notion that it springs also from the instinct for harmony and rhythm suggests poetic obliquity. When a man feels keenly about an event it is natural that he should talk about it in verse; and if he does not feel too keenly he will be content to dwell on the mere event and to stick to the emotions connected with it.

One of the uses of direct poetry therefore is to state, and by stating to digest, experiences as they arise. Milton's sonnet written on his twenty-third birthday ('How soon hath Time . . .') deals directly with his anxiety at being so slow in positive achievement. It is all the more clearly direct because it was appended to a prose letter to an unknown friend on the same topic. The present experience is the main concern, and Milton resorts to verse not because of any alien matters inexpressible in prose but because only through verse can he state his experience to his own satisfaction. Chaucer's description of the poor parson in the Prologue to the *Canterbury Tales* may be this kind of poetry. It makes no difference whether or not he had an actual person in mind. Chaucer was moved by the experience of noting such virtue in the midst of so much vice or mediocrity, and he digested his experience by giving the best account he could of what he had noted.

Sometimes direct poetry of this kind will take an elaborate form. Yeats's *The Tower* is an example. For all its embroidery it deals primarily with actual personal experiences and with contemporary politics, the mention of Burke and Grattan being the focusing point of the whole poem:

> It is time that I wrote my will;
> I choose upstanding men
> That climb the streams until
> The fountain leap, and at dawn
> Drop their cast at the side
> Of dripping stone; I declare
> They shall inherit my pride,
> The pride of people that were
> Bound neither to Cause nor to State,
> Neither to slaves that were spat on,
> Nor to the tyrants that spat,
> The people of Burke and of Grattan
> That gave, though free to refuse.

Yeats's poem is dated, it refers closely to the time when it was written, in no less a degree than Milton's sonnet.

Meredith's *Modern Love* is a poem of re-enactment through direct statement. It is full of ingenuities but they all point towards the professed subject. Take the thirty-fourth section:

> Madam would speak with me. So, now it comes:
> The Deluge or else Fire! She's well; she thanks
> My husbandship. Our chain on silence clanks.
> Time leers between, above his twiddling thumbs.
> Am I quite well? Most excellent in health!

The journals, too, I diligently peruse.
Vesuvius is expected to give news:
Niagara is no noisier.   By stealth
Our eyes dart scrutinizing snakes.   She's glad
I'm happy, says her quivering under-lip.
'And are not you?' 'How can I be?' 'Take ship!
For happiness is somewhere to be had.'
'Nowhere for me!' Her voice is barely heard.
I am not melted, and make no pretence.
With commonplace I freeze her, tongue and sense.
Niagara or Vesuvius is deferred.

Here the poet is mainly occupied with the actual happening, whether as reflecting his own experience or as typify-
ing things that do happen.   And if we allow ourselves to
embroider on the poem we do not stray from its context,
going no further away from it than to think 'Meredith
must have suffered agony himself to write like that.'   Any
notion that the situation symbolises something else is
ludicrous.

So much for one large kind of direct poetry: the kind
which deals primarily with an actual happening either
physical or mental, which gets its value for the author
through ordering the happening, and which is relevant to
the reader because the happening and its ordering are not
just private to the author but could occur at any time or
place and to any normal person.

There is a second and copious kind of direct poetry that
does not refer to any actual experience but expounds a
doctrine or expresses general moral ideas.   Dryden's
Religio Laici expounds doctrines in which he was interested
enough to versify them but not interested enough to trans-
mute into oblique form.   Johnson's *Vanity of Human Wishes*
expresses directly moral ideas about which he felt strongly
but for whose transmutation into oblique form he did not
possess the technical skill.   There is also a mass of verse expressing conventional and not very deeply held doctrines
or moral ideas which on the whole can be thought of as

direct poetry. The Middle Ages produced plenty of this kind. Here is a passage chosen at random from Gower's *Confessio Amantis*: [1]

> First whan the highe god began
> This worlde and that the kind of man
> Was fall into no gret encress,
> For worldes good was tho no press,
> But all was set to the comune.
> They speken than of no fortune
> Or for to lese or for to winne,
> Till avarice brought it in.
> And that was whan the world was woxe
> Of man, of hors, of shepe, of oxe,   10

---

[1] Book 5, 1-57. 'When God on high first set the world going and mankind was not yet very numerous, there was no competition for worldly weath, but everything went to the common store. Men never spoke then of fortune, whether gain or loss was in question, till avarice brought in the custom. And that was when the world had grown in men, horses, sheep, and oxen, and when men got to know of money. Then peace departed, and war came in on every side, which thrust out all love and turned the common store into private property. So that instead of the shovel and spade the sharp sword was taken up. And in this way the occasion arose whence men made deep ditches and high walls to protect the gold hoarded tight by avarice. But the avaricious man, though he might buy the world, considers it all too little. Therefore, all the gold, cattle, or land he can grasp he never lets go again, but gets more and holds it fast, as if the world would last for ever. In this he resembles hell; for, as the old books say, what comes in there, in small or great quantity, shall never get out again. Thus when he has locked his money-chest it shall never be unfastened except when he wants to see how bright his gold shines, so that he can look and gloat over it. Apart from this he dare have no habitual share in it, big or small. Thus he is poor and ever lacks that of which he has plenty. An ox pulls along the plough and gets no reward for his toil. A sheep is in the same case; he carries the wool, but one day another takes away the fleece. In the same way the avaricious man possesses so that he does not possess at all, for he takes no part of his possession. For anyone with a decent understanding it is impertinent to say that a man like this possesses wealth. That wealth possesses *him* and holds him bound, so that he gets no pleasure from it but is its slave. Thus he serves as a subject when he ought to be master. Such is the generation of the avaricious.'

And that men knewen the money.
Tho wente pees out of the wey
And werre came on every side,
Which alle love laid aside
And of comun his propre made;
So that in stede of shovel and spade
The sharpe swerd was take on honde.
And in this wise it cam to londe,
Wherof men maden diches depe
And highe walles for to kepe 20
The gold, which avarice encloseth.
But all to litel supposeth,
Though he might all the world purchase.
For what thing, that he may embrace
Of golde, of catel, or of londe,
He let it never out of his honde,
But get him more and halt it fast,
As though the world shuld ever last.
So is he lich unto the helle,
For as these olde bokes telle, 30
What cometh ther in lass or more
It shall departe nevermore.
Thus whan he hath his cofre loken,
It shall nought after ben unstoken
But whan him list to have a sight
Of gold how that it shineth bright,
That he theron may loke and muse;
For otherwise he dare nought use
To take his part or lasse or more.
So is he pouer, and evermore 40
Him lacketh that he hath inough.
An oxe draweth in the plough,
Of that him self hath no profite;
A shep right in the same plite
His wolle bereth, but on a day
An other taketh the flees away.
Thus hath he that he nought ne hath,
For he therof his part ne tath.

To say how such a man hath good,
Who so that reson understood,   50
It is unproperliche said.
That good hath him and halt him taid,
That he no gladdeth nought withall
But is unto his good a thrall,
And a subgit thus serveth he
Where that he shulde maister be.
Such is the kinde of thavarous.

Here the tone is social and not passionately individual, for the sentiment, though sincerely acquiesced in, is derivative and would earn the readiest nominal acceptance from men in society: no sense of the poet's springing unpleasant surprises on the plain man; for what man of the world does not agree that the person who hoards his wealth is a fool or even a knave? The craft is consummate and yet it promotes strictly the matter in hand. The passage is constructed on the simple but effective rhetorical design of exposition (lines 1-41), illustration (42-8), and conclusion. *Avarice* is the subject, and the word is introduced with sounding emphasis in line 8, reintroduced powerfully but in a different position in line 21, while the passage ends with its adjectival form: enough emphasis to be effective without being intrusive. The rhythm is beautifully manipulated to make vivid the sense of the words. In line 7 it is poised delicately in a doubt: win or lose meant nothing to those men; not a grain in the scales either way. In the next line *avarice* upsets the balance with a crash. The quick enumeration in line 10 makes you multiply the beasts; there are lots of them all at once. In lines 13 and 17 *werre* and *swerd* sound with cruel emphasis. There is a horrified stillness about 'As though the world shuld ever last' (line 28), implying 'as if *anyone* could *think* of such a thing.' Line 32 expresses a solemn finality. And last, in line 52 the monosyllables, especially the first four, hammer home the conclusion with firm rhetorical skill and betoken an appropriate flicker up of feeling.

I have dwelt on this passage from Gower, because it illustrates some typical marks of direct poetry, more especially of the direct poetry that expounds a doctrine or expresses general moral ideas. Three of these marks may be mentioned.

First, the excellence of the craft shows up the more through the very absence of passion. As the mind has its faculties less fiercely strained than in reading the more complicated kinds, so it has the more leisure to be conscious of the medium. All poetry is more or less oblique; and the chief obliquity of this less oblique kind consists in what the sheer craft expresses. Through careful diction and honest structure this poetry can imply a protest that 'English must be kept up,' that verse below a certain technical standard must not be tolerated; that you cannot get something for nothing and that sound work is its own reward. These are sentiments that we can assimilate in our less intense moods, when we are unfit for the highest kinds of poetry; and the verse that conveys them is not on that account to be despised. It may indeed tend sometimes to bore us; but, if the boredom is of the right kind, that does not matter.

Secondly, the poetry of statement, such as this passage from Gower, has a clearer social function than much poetry of a higher order; it deals naturally with the normal psychology of social man. With the greatest moral truths the poetry of statement cannot adequately cope. These have to be lived or relived from the beginning; and the poet who has passed through any so transforming experience will find directness unsuitable to the state of mind he has reached. But the small social and moral commonplaces, the more quotidian of the human passions, pass easily into direct statement. Some of the best of Browning is of this kind.

> But bless you it's dear—it's dear! fowls, wine, at double the
> rate.
> They have clapped a new tax upon salt, and what oil pays
> passing the gate

It's a horror to think of. And so, the villa for me, not the
city!
Beggars can scarcely be choosers—but still—ah, the pity,
the pity!

Many of the epistles of the seventeenth century are sound
and agreeable social verse and have a human warmth
about them absent from the austerer modes. Byron in
Beppo and *Don Juan* has delightful pieces of social observation directly stated, as in this description of Lambro re-
turning to his island and finding Don Juan and Haidée:

> Perhaps you think in stumbling on this feast
>   He flew into a passion, and in fact
> There was no mighty reason to be pleased;
>   Perhaps you prophesy some sudden act,
> The whip, the rack, or dungeon at the least,
>   To teach his people to be more exact,
> And that, proceeding at a very high rate,
> He show'd the royal *penchants* of a pirate.
>
> You're wrong.—He was the mildest manner'd man
>   That ever scuttled ship or cut a throat;
> With such true breeding of a gentleman,
>   You never could divine his real thought;
> No courtier could, and scarcely woman can
>   Gird more deceit into a petticoat;
> Pity he loved adventurous life's variety,
> He was so great a loss to good society.

Some of the best-known passages of Shakespeare are of this
social kind, for Shakespeare was not at all above mixing
minor directnesses with major obliquities. 'All the
world's a stage' is a good enough example. Here it is no
great moral truth, won by deep personal experience, that
he expresses, but the kind of observation any of us might
attain to. He expresses it with perfectly sound craft. The
result is something not beyond the reach of men in their
more gregarious moods.

Thirdly, the passage of Gower is mediocre poetry that serves to set off the superior kinds. It is doubtful if we can get the full force of the best verse without having the humbler kinds as a standard of comparison. A long poem like *The Iliad* supplies within itself its own background; Pindar gained by the discovery of Bacchylides; Chaucer gains if Gower is not forgotten. Direct poetry will thus correspond to the sheer observation of manners and of mind that fills the bulk of some of the greatest novels and which prepares for their crucial episodes. Ever since Poe pronounced that a long poem was a series of short genuine poems united by long stretches of stuff that was not poetry at all, people have been apt to slight this humble but necessary function of direct poetry. It is better to accept the necessity and to recognise and enjoy the pleasures that the humble types of poetry have to offer.

2. REINFORCED AND EMBROIDERED STATEMENT

Let us now move along the scale towards obliquity and consider the more ambitious forms of statement. There must be a large body of transitional verse, but none the less should one apply to it wherever possible the test of statement or obliquity; for much apparently elaborate verse may on examination turn out to be fundamentally statement; and much apparently less elaborate, fundamentally oblique. And the dangers of applying wrong standards are as genuine near the frontiers as in the undisputed territories, and certainly more subtle. The principle dividing reinforced or embroidered statement from obliquity has already been hinted at through what was said in the last chapter about *The Tower* and *Modern Love*: when rhythm and metaphor do no more than reinforce or embroider statement, then we have the poetry of statement still; when rhythm or metaphor imply something behind the statement, something additional or alien to it, then obliquity begins. In the same way true allegory belongs to statement. It does not consist of something behind the statement, but it is something put in front of the statement, something which by interposing a temporary obfuscation serves to make the statement more interesting or more emphatic. It is obvious that this distinction gives endless material of dispute when specific poems are criticised; but it is not thereby invalidated.

The nature of reinforced statement can be conveniently observed in the practice of onomatopoeia. Here the sound of the verse is made to back up the sound implied by the intellectual content of the words. In

> The Trumpets loud Clangor
>   Excites us to Arms
> With shrill Notes of Anger
>   And mortal Alarms.
> The double double double beat
>   Of the thund'ring Drum,
> Cryes, heark the Foes come;
> Charge, charge, 'tis too late to retreat,

the sound of the words skilfully urges us to notice their intellectual content; but it does nothing to take us behind it. The only obliquity of the passage is the one already mentioned as common to most good poetry of statement: the belief in sound technique, in the virtue of taking trouble and of turning out good work. Dryden, you feel, has done his job thoroughly in this passage; and he knows it; like God the craftsman, he sees that his work is good. The reason why onomatopoeic verse has been unduly cried up and (in recent days) cried down is that it has been judged by excessive standards. The awesome praise once bestowed on such examples as Tennyson's cooing doves and murmuring bees suggested mysterious value in the device, while some recent reactions against it have been overcharged with virtuous indignation. Looked on as a humble but useful minister to the poetry of statement, onomatopoeia need not rouse in us any very violent passions. That is, if it does not pass into obliquity; for then it both passes from its own proper realm and competes for praise on different grounds. Take Virgil's description in the sixth book of *The Aeneid* of getting wood for Misenus's burial:

> Itur in antiquam silvam, stabula alta ferarum;
> procumbunt piceae; sonat icta securibus ilex;
> fraxineaeque trabes cuneis et fissile robur
> scinditur; advolvunt ingentes montibus ornos.[1]

This is onomatopoeic verse: Virgil has got the crash of falling trees, the ring of the axe, the split of timber very successfully into his verse. In particular the four words 'sonat icta securibus ilex' suggest the rhythmic ring of the axes, with their woodland echo, to perfection. But, unlike Dryden's lines, their significance extends beyond their statement-reference. Something more has got into them; perhaps prompted by the thought of the beasts in the previous line. It might be some primitive horror of lurking dangers, or some ecstasy induced by the sunny spots of greenery in a glade. But the words are oblique, as Dryden's lines are direct; and we do them an injustice to confine their value to the humble function of onomatopoeia.

By calling unmixed onomatopoeia humble I do not wish to imply that the poetry of statement, when reinforced to the utmost, cannot be very good or even great. For an example of very literal statement raised by emphasis to great poetry take some lines from a poem by Blake, written in the autumn of 1801, sent in a letter to William Butts and sometimes known by the title of *Los the Terrible*. Though containing some minor obscurities, in the main the poem recounts straightforwardly the poet's troubles at the time of writing and his defiance of the worst that the world can do to him. It seemed impossible to poor Blake to please Hayley without offending Butts, or to do the right thing by his wife and his sister at the same time. And in general,

---

[1] 'They pass into the ancient forest, the deep coverts of game; pitchpines fall flat, ilex rings to the strokes of axes, and ashen beams and oak are split in clefts with wedges; they roll in huge mountain-ashes from the hills.' (Mackail's translation.)

temporal conditions, symbolised in this poem by Los, seemed too much for him:

> The curses of Los, the terrible shade,
> And his dismal terrors make me afraid.

And then Blake, with his double vision, instead of the 'Mild sun that mounts and sings' early in the poem, sees Los in the sun. And at the sight he defies him in these words:

> My hands are labour'd day and night,
> And Ease comes never in my sight.
> My Wife has no indulgence given
> Except what comes to her from heaven.
> We eat little, we drink less;
> This Earth breeds not our happiness.
> Another Sun feeds our life's streams,
> We are not warmed with thy beams;
> Thou measurest not the Time to me,
> Nor yet the Space that I do see;
> My Mind is not with thy light array'd,
> Thy terrors shall not make me afraid.

The passage means no more than it states, but it states a great deal, and the rhythm backs the statement so surely that to demand anything different, to exact obliquity, would be monstrous. The statement,

> We eat little, we drink less;
> This Earth breeds not our happiness,

is the simplest of literal truths—Blake and his wife were very spare in diet and they had no worldly success—but poetically it is of a very high order.

An admirable example of statement adorned is Shirley's 'The glories of our blood and state.' It is number 288 in *The Oxford Book of English Verse*; and if anyone wants a minor metaphysical obliquity to compare with it he can find it on the opposite page of the same book in Carew's

STATEMENT

'Ask me no more where Jove bestows.' As a love-poem, which it purports to be, Carew's song is a very indifferent piece of hyperbole. But it is a good poem in its small way, and its virtues must be sought outside its nominal reference. Shirley's on the other hand is a genuine moralising poem. He has accepted the great commonplace of pride being levelled by death, he has acquiesced in it: and the poem's excellence consists in the skill with which he has emphasised, adorned, and developed the thought.

> The glories of our blood and state
>   Are shadows, not substantial things,
> There is no armour against fate,
>   Death lays his icy hand on Kings;
>   Scepter and Crown
>   Must tumble down,
> And in the dust be equal made
> With the poor crooked sithe and spade.
>
> Some men with swords may reap the field,
>   And plant fresh laurels where they kill:
> But their strong nerves at last must yield;
>   They tame but one another still:
>   Early or late
>   They stoop to fate,
> And must give up their murmuring breath
> When they pale Captives creep to death.
>
> The Garlands wither on your brow,
>   Then boast no more your mighty deeds;
> Upon Death's purple Altar now
>   See where the Victor-victim bleeds.
>   Your heads must come
>   To the cold Tomb:
> Only the actions of the just
> Smell sweet, and blossom in their dust.

The poem is thick with metaphors, yet every metaphor gets heeded to the full. It needed skill to prevent their quarrelling and to get them firmly chained into the phalanx. And vivid as most of them are, they rarely set the imagination off on distant quests but serve rather to support the acknowledged argument. For a moment the 'poor crooked sithe and spade' with their suggestion of the peasant, wielder of these tools, being likewise bent and worn with toil open a vista away from the pomp of power; but the poet cleverly closes it by his agricultural metaphor 'reap the field' in the next line. 'No,' he says in effect, 'you must think of the agricultural implement, not of the men who use it.' The general tone of the metre, varied though it is by the short couplet within each stanza, is that of enunciation, not of suggestion. The first four lines of the third stanza make one think of Byron's ringing protests and especially of *The Isles of Greece*, whose rhythms they have anticipated to perfection. For all its richness Shirley's lyric looks forward to the directness of the Augustans. So considered it is a noble poem; to apply to it the standards of Marvell's *To his Coy Mistress* is to misunderstand it and to find it defective.

Shelley's *Alastor* will now serve both to provide examples of allegory as an embroidery of statement and to demonstrate how important it is to know whether it is statement or obliquity with which we have to deal. One reason why *Alastor* is such a puzzling poem and, as a whole, so unsatisfactory is that statement and obliquity are difficult to disentangle. At one time Shelley's descriptions of rivers and caves seem to be no more than heightened records of things seen: at another they explicitly symbolise some mental experience. But to decide exactly when description ends and obliquity begins is impossible. To complicate things still more, Shelley introduces an element of undoubted allegory, and of allegory ornamented to the highest degree: to such a degree that one cannot be certain that ornamentation does not become the most important element and force the poetry into the realm of obliquity. The passage I mean is lines 67 to 128, where the poet's youth and early wanderings are described.

STATEMENT

Here the geographical wanderings are the appropriate allegorical substitute for the mental adventures of a young man in search of knowledge and truth, and of a young man with a marked likeness to Shelley:

> When early youth had passed, he left
> His cold fireside and alienated home
> To seek strange truths in undiscovered lands.

Some of his studies are scientific:

> Nature's most secret steps
> He like her shadow has pursued, where'er
> The red volcano overcanopies
> Its fields of snow and pinnacles of ice
> With burning smoke.

Astronomy too occupied him, and finally he recounts how he had ransacked early history for its secrets:

> His wandering step
> Obedient to high thoughts, has visited
> The awful ruins of the days of old:
> Athens, and Tyre, and Balbec, and the waste
> Where stood Jerusalem, the fallen towers
> Of Babylon, the eternal pyramids,
> Memphis and Thebes, and whatsoe'er of strange
> Sculptured on alabaster obelisk,
> Or jasper tomb, or mutilated sphynx,
> Dark Aethiopia in her desert hills
> Conceals.

For all its elaboration of details this is the poetry of statement. Shelley is telling us about his own reading: his version of what Hogg tells about him in *Shelley at Oxford*. Though a little over-Miltonised, the verse is sound; good statement made more interesting by allegorical embroidery. We know where we are with it, and it is an admirable taking-off place. (Or, if you like, it is ready to form part of a larger obliquity.) Unfortunately Shelley

never makes it clear where he does take off. His poet's
further wanderings lack any certain meaning:

> The Poet wandering on, through Arabie
> And Persia, and the wild Carmanian waste,
> And o'er the aërial mountains which pour down
> Indus and Oxus from their icy caves,
> In joy and exultation held his way;
> Till in the vale of Cashmire, far within
> Its loneliest dell, where odorous plants entwine
> Beneath the hollow rocks a natural bower,
> Beside a sparkling rivulet he stretched
> His languid limbs.

Here the allegory ceases. Though we could admit the
Poet's dabbling in Arabic and Persian lore as the meaning
of his wandering 'through Arabie and Persia,' the wild
Carmanian waste is too much for us, and from Indus and
Oxus we can scarcely coax a cultural significance. What
have we then here? Fanciful description for description's
sake, or symbolism? Is the bower a symbol of some recess
of human thought? The rhythm is in no way heightened:
nothing to suggest the deeper vein of symbolism. Yet in this
bower he has a vision, and in the fine description of how
the earth looked when he waked from it, he seems to use
the moon as a fixed symbol of lifelessness and disillusion:

> Roused by the shock he started from his trance—
> The cold white light of morning, the blue moon
> Low in the west, the clear and garish hills,
> The distant valley and the vacant woods,
> Spread round him where he stood. Whither have fled
> The hues of heaven that canopied his bower
> Of yesternight? The sounds that soothed his sleep,
> The mystery and the majesty of Earth,
> The joy, the exultation? His wan eyes
> Gaze on the empty scene as vacantly
> As ocean's moon looks on the moon in heaven.

Not only has allegory given way to symbolism, but the

whole passage is oblique. The last line does not merely reinforce the wanness of the Poet's eyes; it expresses obliquely the experience of spiritual aridity—and with what power! Could Shelley have made such undoubted obliquities spring from the undoubted directness of the passage describing his youthful studies, he would have given the poem a force it lacks as a whole. Much of it, unfortunately, is in the indeterminate mode of the fourth quotation. *Alastor* illustrates copiously the borderland of statement and obliquity.

3. DISGUISED STATEMENT

It is perfectly legitimate for statement to dress itself up even to a high pitch of elaboration, provided it does not pretend to be oblique. But it has no business to masquerade as obliquity. When statement commits this crime, I call it disguised statement. Obviously it is at a time when obliquity is fashionable that such a crime is most often committed; and examples are found most freely in the later Metaphysical period and to-day. Cowley's *Mistress* is full of disguised statement. Cowley had a clever logical and well-trained mind, and a strong social sense. He was admirably suited to write poetry of statement. But owing to the Metaphysical fashion, he must needs fabricate obliquities to which nothing in his mind corresponded. The virtues that his *Mistress* uniformly exhibits, good sense and argumentative skill, he painfully overlays with would-be subtleties. The following is a poem called *Separation*:

> Ask me not what my love shall do or be
> (Love which is soul to body and soul of me)
> When I am separated from thee.
> Alas, I might as easily show
> What after death the soul will do;
> 'Twill last, I'm sure, and that is all we know.

32

The thing called soul will never stir nor move,
But all that while a lifeless carcass prove,
   For 'tis the body of my love;
   Not that my love will fly away,
But still continue as, they say,
Sad troubled ghosts about their graves do stray.

The poet fairly advertises his obliquity. The notion that love is the very soul of the soul should express some very rare mental state; and it does nothing of the sort: it has a faint interest to the poet as part of an argument in which he takes just enough interest to enable him to endure the labour of composing a dozen sluggish lines. It is vain to multiply examples from the seventeenth century: they abound in the weaker metaphysical verse.

Mallarmé in his *Divagations relativement au vers* pronounced uncompromisingly against all statement in poetry and for pure obliquity:

> Un désir indéniable à ce temps est de séparer comme en vue d'attributions différentes le double état de la parole, brut ou immédiat ici, là essentiel.

Poetry is never concerned with the physical properties of things.

> Abolie, la prétention, esthétiquement une erreur, malgré qu'elle régit presque tous les chefs-d'œuvre, d'inclure au papier subtil du volume autre chose que par exemple l'horreur de la forêt, ou le tonnerre muet épars au feuillage: non le bois intrinsèque et dense des arbres. Quelques jets de l'intime orgueil véridiquement trompetés éveillent l'architecture du palais, le seul habitable; hors de toute pierre, sur quoi les pages se refermeraient mal.

A good deal of recent English verse has accepted Mallarmé's doctrine and the obligation to be oblique at any cost; with the result that some of it, naturally belonging to the province of statement, masquerades as obliquity; and among the more serious practitioners as well as among the Enoch Soameses.

c   33

STATEMENT

In Eliot's ambitious and erudite *Gerontion* there is a passage where the obliquity wears very thin:

> After such knowledge, what forgiveness? Think now
> History has many cunning passages, contrived corridors
> And issues, deceives with whispering ambitions,
> Guides us by vanities. Think now
> She gives when our attention is distracted
> And what she gives, gives with such supple confusions
> That the giving famishes the craving. Gives too late
> What's not believed in, or if still believed,
> In memory only, reconsidered passion. Gives too soon
> Into weak hands, what's thought can be dispensed with
> Till the refusal propagates a fear.

Here the verse, elaborately imitated from Tourneur or some other late Elizabethan dramatist (the words 'the giving famishes the craving' have an air of pastiche about them, unless they are an actual quotation), suggests some subtle state of mind. But no amount of re-reading or goodwill has revealed anything at all subtle. On the contrary, all this talk about history reminds one of the author's essay on *Tradition and the Individual Talent*, and the post-Elizabethan form is the inappropriate and laboriously wrought receptacle of ideas already existing: disguised statement, a bogus obliquity.

Ezra Pound's *Hugh Selwyn Mauberley* is full of disguised statement. Pound with his erudition, his patient experiments, and his consistent belief in the virtue of poetry as a craft, is well qualified to turn out competent poetry of statement. But plainly he has other ambitions for himself; he must achieve obliquity; and he tries to do so by stifling statement with all sorts of ingenuities. This is how he ends the first poem of the series (*E. P. Ode pour l'élection de son sépulcre*). He is describing his own literary history:

> His true Penelope was Flaubert,
> He fished by obstinate isles;

34

DISGUISED STATEMENT

Observed the elegance of Circe's hair
Rather than the mottoes on sundials.

Unaffected by 'the march of events'
He passed from men's memory in *l'an trentiesme*
De son eage; the case presents
No adjunct to the Muses' diadem.

This is too pretentious, its literary reference and circumlocutions are too laboured for it to fall into the class of
embroidered statement. It aims higher and it fails. The
metaphors are mere translations of statement, bringing up
the mind short with a jerk. The mottoes on sundials move
us no more than the simpler 'flight of time'; and the
phrase 'adjunct to the Muses' diadem' is no more interesting than the common circumlocutions of the daily press.
The reference to Villon in *l'an trentiesme de son eage* is more
bogus obliquity. The poet is elaborately parading his
pretended failure to achieve poetic distinction and slips in
the quotation to make us contrast him with Villon, who,
though an unregenerate café-loafer, did succeed in writing poetry: would-be obliquity through allusion. But for
all the heat it engenders, the sentiment might have been
put in the baldest prose. The versification is certainly a
clever attempt to transplant some of the rhythms of
Gautier's *Emaux et Camées* into English: but even this has
the air of being plastered on; it is utterly inorganic.

This is not to deny what was said above about Pound's
virtues; only he might have been better advised to be less
ambitious, frankly embroidering statement and not aiming
at obliquities which his not very distinguished mental experiences do not justify. And if this applied to Ezra
Pound, it applied to some lesser men too.

OBLIQUITY

I. THE SPHERE OF OBLIQUITY

IT would seem at first sight ridiculous to treat this topic because of the difficulty of limiting the sphere of obliquity. Can any of the experiences that lend themselves to creating poetry, it may be asked, be denied the possibility of oblique expression? Yet some sort of order seems possible, for many of the oblique meanings that can be detected in poetry do group themselves under certain headings. And though I can do no more than indicate a few of these headings, these may serve as samples of the kind of significance that may underlie or emerge from matters that may not at first seem to concern it.

(i) Sensibility

We now take it for granted that a poet is a man of unusual sensibility. Is there any call, then, to mention such obvious material for oblique rendering? There is ; because sensibility has been taken mainly as the poet's endowment, as his prerequisite for expressing something else, and not as the material of his verse. Actually, there is a large amount of verse whose main subject-matter is a superior sensibility and whose value to the reader consists in communicating a sensibility superior to his own. When a poet is great in other things as well, it may seem superfluous to criticise him in terms of sensibility. But when a poet's sensibility is his chief or sole virtue, analysis of that quality at once becomes crucial in criticism. Moreover there are many poets of this order ; I suspect indeed that most minor poets are of it ; sensibility is the main material of such obliquity as they achieve.

SENSIBILITY

A reason for neglecting sensibility as a theme of poetry is the very natural present-day reaction against its abuses in the eighteenth and nineteenth centuries. But we should not submit weakly to the simple error of confusing the thing and the abuse of it. Most people would be better for a heightened and more varied capacity to feel ; and a most legitimate function of poetry is to heighten that capacity. We must not be put off by the effusiveness of much minor verse written in the last century, but must remember two things : first, that not all would-be sensitive verse shows much sensibility ; second, that sensibility was the main material of many poems long before the senti-mental movement of the eighteenth century. What cheap-ened sensibility was the habit of describing it directly by its symptoms instead of expressing it obliquely through the various parts of the poem. Some of the great Romantic poets indeed described the symptoms admirably, but they left a method far too easily imitable by anyone who fancied himself more sensitive than his fellows. Poems of pure sensibility are rare till the age of Elizabeth, but from then on there are many in which the qualities other than sensi-bility are negligible except for keeping that quality healthily balanced. However ludicrous it may sound to discuss Shakespeare's general sensibility, an early poem like *Venus and Adonis* gets most of its value from the mental poten-tiality that constitutes that quality. Drummond of Haw-thornden is a minor poet from whose verse the sense of an exquisite sensibility emerges. I doubt whether he had any other remarkable mental quality. Much the same is true of some Elizabethan sonnet-sequences. It is difficult to criticise either Drummond or these sequences in terms of sensibility ; but nothing of value is likely to be said of them in any other terms.

Possibly very little *can* be said on the matter, but that little would be more apt than the mere enumeration of external characteristics of which criticism of such poetry usually consists. We are told, for instance, of the 'mar-vellous accuracy of Tennyson's nature-descriptions' or of the 'exquisite delicacy of Pope's *Rape of the Lock*.' Now both these are examples of poetry whose virtue *mainly* depends on the peculiar sensibility they express. The phrase about Tennyson suggests that his nature-descriptions are valuable because they stir in us the recollection of those things they treat of. Thomson's *Seasons* may be a poem largely of this kind. But some of Tennyson's descriptions have little purely descriptive substance nor do they show a cool, scientific accuracy, but an altogether more complicated phenomenon. For instance, in the middle of the dreary narrative of *Geraint and Enid* Tennyson suddenly wakes up the reader with these lines:

> So thro' the green gloom of the wood they past,
> And issuing under open heavens beheld
> A little town with towers, upon a rock,
> And close beneath, a meadow gemlike chased
> In the brown wild, and mowers mowing in it.

It does not get one far to call this a Pre-Raphaelite picture (as one is immediately tempted to do), but at least it is better to call it this than a realistic description. What is certain is that here is an obliquity. The sudden picture of the airy little town and the unnaturally bright meadow and the unreal mowers has little to do with actual life but is an immediate concrete rendering of a mood or an idea. It is the strange, perhaps over-acute sensibility that constitutes the virtue of the passage. *The Rape of the Lock* offers the spectacle of one of the rarest and most quiveringly alive sensibilities possessed by any poet, elegantly and successfully masquerading under an objective poetical form. The sensibility is nearly everything. The moral of the poem, the preaching, through not too violent satire, of moderation and reasonableness, is shadowy. What matters is the fierce though tenuous apprehension of the doings of the fashionable life. The trivialities have for the superior sensibility of Pope an almost devastating glamour and excitement.

For lo! the board with cups and spoons is crown'd,
The berries crackle, and the mill turns round;
On shining Altars of Japan they raise
The silver lamp; the fiery spirits blaze:
From silver spouts the grateful liquors glide,
While China's earth receives the smoking tide.

Pope is of course steadied by the fine early eighteenth century convention of the burlesque epic, but what makes this passage so unusual, what raises it so far above the trivial, is the hypertrophied sensibility that for all the apparent control is shaken to its depths by the tiniest happenings of everyday life.

Sensibility, then, we may expect to be a very frequent subject of oblique expression; and it is likely to be most truly present when least is said about it. And it may so easily be missed, for there is a large body of verse that seeks to express sensibility with an obvious, often a brutal directness, and tends to obscure the oblique expression of that quality. Unless the poet says, 'I feel, I feel,' we are apt to look for qualities other than pure sensibility in his verse. We should be sceptical of such protests and look for sensibility in its subtler manifestations.

(ii) The Great Commonplaces

The quest for obliquity in the large general features of poetry has been badly hindered by much talk about the 'passions.' Ever since Aristotle defined tragedy as the imitation of an action (which of course for him was not confined to the physical) and brought in pity and fear, most critics have omitted to ask whether such an imitation were means or end, and the usual result has been to assume that it is the latter. Lisideius, in Dryden's *Essay of Dramatic Poesy*, defined a play as 'a just and lively image of human nature, representing its passions and humours, and the changes of fortune to which it is subject, for the delight and instruction of mankind.' Here it is assumed that the mere representation is an end; it delights and instructs in itself. Arnold, speaking of all the larger types of poetry, thinks the same. He says:

> What are the eternal objects of Poetry, among all nations and at all times? They are actions; human actions; possessing an inherent interest in themselves, and which are to be communicated in an interesting manner by the art of the Poet. . . . And what actions are the most excellent? Those, certainly, which most powerfully appeal to the great primary human affections: to those elementary feelings which subsist permanently in the race, and which are independent of time. . . . Poetical works belong to the domain of our permanent passions: let them interest these, and the voice of all subordinate claims upon them is at once silenced.

Once it was believed that the great poetical forms had no more to do than to exhibit the great passions in an interesting way, criticism was bound to hunt down those passions; in fact to become psychological. Hence Morgann's essay on Falstaff and the 'character' criticism of the nineteenth century. This criticism tacitly assumes that a convincing picture of the 'great primary human affections' is a poetic end in itself, and that if the critic penetrates the various psychological shadows that cannot but obscure any complicated picture, he has, rhapsody apart, done all that can be asked of him. The major forms of poetry therefore were reduced to a highly concentrated form of direct statement. The poet said things about human passions, or explained human nature; and that sufficed: it was not the habit to ask whether these passions were the means to any further significance, whether they were figures of some pattern larger than themselves. It is not that the nineteenth century critics were wrong in discussing psychology. If, as Coleridge said so often, Othello is credulous rather than jealous according to the evidence of the play, it is well to realise the fact: it is one that may have its bearing on the play's ultimate meaning. The error is to think that criticism can stop when it has proved that Othello is less jealous than credulous. What it should go on to do is to decide whether it is concerned with statement or with obliquity, whether the poem in question is merely 'a just and lively image of human nature, representing its passions and humours,' or whether these passions exist less for their own sake than for an ulterior significance. For it is possible to make this distinction. *Aurora Leigh* has merit chiefly because it is—in part at least—'a just and lively image of human nature,' but that image has no ulterior importance, its function stops there. Can one possibly limit *Paradise Lost* in this way? And so with Browning's *Men and Women* compared with *Much Ado About Nothing* or *The Way of the World*. If it has been decided that the poem or play is oblique, criticism of the 'passions' should take a subordinate place, and the main task should be to answer the question of what the obliquity is.

It will be convenient here to recall my remarks on Blake's *Echoing Green*. Brief as that poem is, it exemplifies the sort of obliquity that often lies behind those passions which bulk so large in the major poetical forms. Granted the interpretation that there is virtue in gratified desire, the poem can be said to express a great human commonplace, and one which in Blake's day more than in our own especially called for expression.

To sum up the profoundest meaning of a great poem by a commonplace has an unpleasant air, bringing art into dangerous proximity to the Wayside Pulpit. And the reason is that the nature of the great commonplaces may easily be misunderstood through being confused with the common run of aphoristic verse. We are apt to think of a scale beginning with such poems as Pope's *Essay on Man* or Herbert's *Church Porch* and descending to Martin Tupper and Wilhelmina Stitch, and to assume that the first two are about as high as the poetry of commonplaces can reach. Actually these two poems are quite on another level than those whose final achievement is to convey a great commonplace. They retail items of religious, moral, or worldly wisdom through direct statement: there

is no question of a single great commonplace being dis-
tilled from all the component parts of the poem. Far from
being akin to the Wayside Pulpit or even to *An Essay on
Man*, the great commonplaces have something mysterious
about them as embodying the utmost wisdom of the race—
and even the Wayside Pulpit with its spiritual ally the
moral calendar, however ineffective their contents, do in
their persistence and ubiquity testify to the deep human
craving for a certain kind of mental food. The great
commonplaces have been gradually captured and con-
solidated through human history; they are the concern of
the whole human race. And it is possible that they were
first expressed in poetry.

Both these notions can be illustrated from the last book
of *The Iliad*.[1] In this book Priam visits Achilles to beg
from him the body of Hector his son, which Achilles has
been abusing by dragging it round the walls of Troy. The
two have every reason to be irreconcilable enemies.
Hector has killed Patroclus, Achilles's second self, and
Achilles not only Hector but many other sons of Priam.
And yet in their common grief they find kinship, and
Priam's request is granted. One can apprehend the last
book of *The Iliad* in different ways. It is an enchanting
picture of life in the heroic age. It could supply the
student of the passions with the most exciting material.
The spectacle of the old and broken king kneeling to
Achilles and kissing the murderer's hands that have been
the death of so many of his sons has been singled out as one
of the most moving incidents in all literature. And the
picture of Achilles's mind during the episode strikes the
reader as so unerringly true to experience that he cannot
believe that there was much about human nature of which
Homer was not aware. And yet it is wrong to stop here,
for there is something behind this poignant exhibition of
the passions. And this is a great commonplace; the idea
that in the utmost extremities the things that unite men

[1] In what follows I am partly indebted to the Epilogue of J. T.
Sheppard's *Pattern of the Iliad*.

are stronger than those that divide them. It was an idea beyond the usual 'heroic' mentality of Homer's day, an imaginative leap beyond the conventional bounds, the scope of whose ramifications it is difficult to limit. In seriousness it far surpasses Pope's aphorisms in *An Essay on Man*, and is nearer akin to the Christian paradox 'Whosoever will save his life shall lose it, and whosoever will lose his life shall find it.'

In the world's history a great commonplace is every now and then brought forth, and poetry may be concerned in its birth; but those that already exist must be kept alive. They are in perpetual danger of perishing. They have to be refelt continually and reformulated by human experience. They cease to be true unless continually ratified by fresh expression. It is one of the functions of poetry, the most intense form of speech, to keep these commonplaces alive, in contemporary idiom, through the ages.

As the great commonplace can be so remote in its origins and so complicated in its history, no direct statement of it is likely to carry weight. We instinctively distrust the man who has the boldness to express one, and we require the most convincing proofs of depth of mind and width of experience before we can overcome our distrust: in fact we require the speaker to talk about most things before saying what he most has to say. We may even prefer the ultimate obliquity of his omitting what he has to say altogether and implying it through an elaborate pattern of seeming irrelevancies.

Conversely in any impressive long poem we may reasonably suspect the presence of one or more great commonplaces. And yet this is often the last thing that is suspected. This is not to say that an impressive long poem *must* contain one; but let the reader consider how much of the criticism of *The Fairy Queen* or *The Prelude* reckons with any such possibility. However correctly a critic draws out the allegory in the one, or analyses Wordsworth's conception of the imagination in the other, he will have left his work incomplete if he has failed to seek out some great common-

43

place diffused through the poem; if, in other words, he has confined the major meaning to direct and not oblique expression.

It is worth while saying more about *The Fairy Queen* and some of its critics, partly to substantiate what I have just said and partly because any important commonplace that the poem may express is pretty certain to be different in kind from Homer's in the last book of *The Iliad.*

Take first Hazlitt's description of Spenser's versification, one of the finest passages from his *Lectures on the English Poets*:

> His versification is at once the most smooth and the most sounding in the language. It is a labyrinth of sweet sounds, 'in many a winding bout of linked sweetness long drawn out,' that would cloy by their very sweetness, but that the ear is constantly relieved and enchanted by their continued variety of modulation, dwelling on the pauses of the action, or flowing on in a fuller tide of harmony with the movement of the sentiment. It has not the bold dramatic transitions of Shakespeare's blank verse, nor the high-raised tone of Milton's; but it is the perfection of melting harmony, dissolving the soul in pleasure, or holding it captive in the chains of suspense. Spenser was the poet of our waking dreams; and he has invented not only a language, but a music of his own for them. The undulations are infinite, like those of the waves of the sea; but the effect is still the same, lulling the senses into a deep oblivion of the jarring noises of the world, from which we have no wish to be ever recalled.

However alien to modern critical methods this passage may be, it cannot be bettered in its way. It presents one of the poetical features of *The Fairy Queen* in the most fascinating light and fulfils the simple critical function of making its reader wish to read or reread the poem it speaks of. It does something which no one whose gift of style falls short of Hazlitt's can possibly hope to do. But for our present purposes what matters is the way Hazlitt assumes he has fulfilled the critic's task: no hint that it might be possible to go on and ask what state of mind or set of ideas this versification expresses.

Next there are the various attempts to explain or to discount the allegory with all its ramifications. Now it is a laudable endeavour to try to settle how far Spenser's allegory should be pushed; and yet those who discuss it usually make the false assumption that it is the fundamental problem in Spenser. Those who find a deep allegorical meaning think it the ultimate meaning, those who find it unimportant think that *The Fairy Queen* has very little meaning at all and that its virtue consists in a charming melody and some brilliant pieces of pageantry. Neither group have carried their inquiries far enough. Allegory is an elaborated form of direct statement: it is a simple substitution designed to stimulate the reader by making him take a little or a great deal of trouble to get at the statement. But when a manifestly important poem is in question, it is not enough to work out the allegory: the problem remains, does the allegorised statement lead to any larger obliquity? Similarly it is wrong to attribute the main virtue of *The Fairy Queen* to pageantry and music, until you have decided that these features do not help to figure forth some large general notion.

Actually, it is an error to isolate the music and the pageantry from the other features of *The Fairy Queen*: from its vastness, its shifting allegories now apparently so significant now so thin, its wealth of learning and historical reference, its unreal air varied by an occasional intrusion of the real world, its blend of melancholy and vitality. Taken with these the characteristic sweetness of Spenser's music and the brilliant unreality of his pageants express not an escape from life but the dissatisfaction he felt with it. He demands of life that it should be better than it actually is, and to say so he both adumbrates the whole pattern of contemporary history and culture and creates an imaginary world in which mundane limitations are quite transcended. He is the fastidious idealist for whom the everyday world can never be good enough. And this idealism is one of the great commonplaces that emerges from the poem. Such a conviction might drive a man, as it did Shelley, to frantic efforts to reform the world. Spenser knew the everyday world too well to react like that. He also had less need to do so, because his age was one of temporary stability. Thus his idealism not only erects a standard of which the world generally falls grievously short but invests with a glamour the things of which he approves: the acts of holiness and courtesy that are performed and the men capable of performing them. In speaking of mutability he not only laments the imperfection of human conditions compared with what they should be but utters his fear lest the things he prizes should be corrupted or destroyed. Such a way of feeling leads to a philosophical conservatism; and this is a second great commonplace that emerges from the poem.

All the above is highly dogmatic and debatable, but at least it is critically an important matter of debate. It really affects Spenser's status as a major or a minor poet.

This reduction of *The Fairy Queen's* ultimate meaning into such prosaic and simple terms must not be allowed to imply that great poetry can be shrivelled to an aphorism. And to avoid making this implication I must enlarge on the nature of the great commonplaces.

The great commonplace in poetry, when obliquely expressed, issues from the various parts of the poem; it is that in which many experiences culminate. And one cannot of course separate the value of a great commonplace from the value of all the complicated experiences that go to creating or rediscovering it. On the contrary, what distinguishes the great commonplace from the mere aphorism is the thoroughness with which it has as it were been lived or relived from the beginning. Its creator takes nothing on trust; he must work through the whole process of creation, as if the data pointed initially to no kind of conclusion. Only on these terms will he get his readers' confidence; and that confidence will apply as much to his experiences as to the commonplace which issues out of them. Unless Homer had lived imaginatively through the normal life of the 'heroic' mind, unless he had entered into the thoughts of all classes of men from the camp-followers to the kings, he would not have been competent to reach his conclusion that the things that unite men are in the last resort more important than those that separate them.

How the emphasis should be divided between the emerging commonplace and the engendering experience will vary according to the reader's temperament. Personally I like to emphasise the commonplace; by so doing I get greater satisfaction from all the parts of a poem. But taste in this matter is bound to differ widely. However, personal differences as to the amount of relative emphasis matter little if it is realised that the commonplace and the experiences are inseparable, that the moral value of the commonplace must depend on the moral value of the experiences.

The kind of moral value involved in the commonplace can be illustrated from the interpretation given to *The Echoing Green*. In Blake's day the commonplace that there is virtue in desire gratified had been moribund since the seventeenth century. It had been overlaid by the other commonplace that gratification of desire leads to anarchy. Blake revived the moribund commonplace. His act had a triple value. He presented to his age an aspect of truth it is perilous to ignore. He also did a service by modifying the commonplace. That is, he recreated it in a form more relevant to his age than its previous form had been. And last, however much Blake's commonplace may be objectified, it has its value as being uniquely his own. Indeed it is through being uniquely his own that its objectification can be trusted, can succeed.

The great commonplaces have a second, supplementary, function. As well as a moral, they have what can be called almost a structural value. They are the merging points of all the other parts of a poem. They react on all those parts and raise them to a value which unaided they would have lacked. Now it is the power of the poet to unite all the parts of his poem into a commonplace that crowns his personal poetical capacity; witness this passage from Coleridge [1]:

> The man that hath not music in his soul can indeed never be a genuine poet. Imagery,—(even taken from nature, much more when transplanted from books, as travels, voyages, and works of natural history),—affecting incidents, just thoughts, interesting personal or domestic feelings, and with these the art of their combination or intertexture in the form of a poem,—may all by incessant effort be acquired as a trade, by a man of talent and much reading, who, as I once before observed, has mistaken an intense desire of poetical reputation for a natural poetical genius; the love of the arbitrary end for a possession of the peculiar means. But the sense of musical delight, with the power of producing it, is a gift of imagination; and this together with the power of reducing multitude into unity of effect, and modifying a series of thoughts by some one predominant thought or feeling, may be cultivated or improved, but can never be learned. It is in these that '*poeta nascitur non fit.*'

In this importance of the commonplace there is an analogy with what I shall say later about Plot. Plot becomes important only as the other poetical features become excellent: when they reach high excellence Plot becomes the most important feature of all. Similarly a unifying commonplace is trivial if the things it unites are mediocre: when those things are already good, their converging into a commonplace produces the final consummation of excellence.

It is ever to be borne in mind that the commonplace must be organic, not something tacked on. It must issue from the sum of all the parts. A mere moral deduced by reason from the incidents of a poem is not the genuine thing. Addison concluded that the moral of *Paradise Lost* was 'that Obedience to the Will of God makes Men

---

[1] *Biographia Literaria*, xv. 1.

happy, and that Disobedience makes them miserable';
and though this may be deduced from the incidents it does
not answer to the impression which all the features of the
poem create; it is inorganic. Simple trust in an Addi-
sonian God whose dictates were easy to ascertain is remote
from the heartsearchings of Milton's poem.

Lastly, it must be borne in mind that the commonplace,
to be of the highest effect, must be powerfully and consistently dominant. Here will be found a criterion
between great and less great poetry. From *The Fairy
Queen* a great commonplace does indeed emerge, but it
does so somewhat faintly and tentatively. It is on re-
flection and with some hesitation that one perceives
Spenser's philosophical conservatism. A greater poet
continuously forces the sense of some great moral truth on
the reader, who is swept away rather than conducts a
careful and deliberate examination. The oblique commonplaces already deduced from *The Echoing Green* and the
twenty-fourth book of *The Iliad*, those I shall define or
suspect in *Prometheus Bound*, *Lycidas*, and *The Miller's Tale*,
are felt throughout their poems and before ever they begin
to give themselves away. They rule their poems and lay
down laws to all those poems' component parts.

(iii) The Primitive

The great commonplaces belong to a fairly complex
stage of human development. Created as they were
through long experience, by comparisons, acceptances and
rejections, they are some way from a dumb instinctive
realisation. There are elements in poetry more primitive
than the great commonplaces, elements much more dimly
illumined by conscious thought. For these, oblique expression was for long the only possible.

Probably the most readily granted of these possible
elements is that of fear. We imagine that in early ages
man was more subject to overwhelming fears than he grew
to be later. When the world around him was so little

touched by his handiwork, when it still seemed capable of wiping him out, there must have existed a general state of fear unknown in later ages. Spasmodic apprehensions of God's bringing the world to an end were quite different from a permanent sense of man's precariousness in a large, perilous, threatening world. That some ballad literature expresses this primal fear, now no longer conscious in us but overlaid rather than erased, is not impossible.

Take another set of primitive feelings. Scholars tell us that the modern idea of progress is of recent origin. Before the seventeenth century it existed very faintly if at all. It began to take shape at the end of that century, grew rapidly in the eighteenth, and reached its zenith in the nineteenth. But the idea of a thing and the experience of it are not the same; and because the idea of progress is recent it does not follow that the joy in it did not count for a great deal in primitive times. If we think of man's primitive fears we must not forget his equally strong joy in making those inventions which, confirming his place in the world, mitigated the ferocity of those very fears. The modern sceptics of progress, in their disillusionment with a recent and over-sanguine theory, give little heed to a primal joy that must have left some deep trace in the mind of man. Superficially it is easy to ridicule the millenarianism of a Shelley, but what if his passion for human betterment is no mere echo of the hopes of his age but the oblique expression of a primal joy hidden in all of us?

But there is a still deeper source of joy, and one which, balanced by an accompanying sorrow, is a much more important source of poetical obliquity. When man was not so far removed from the animals but was emerging into self-consciousness, he must have been animated by an intense relish of achievement. The vitality that drove him to know himself must during achievement have given him a rich return of excited joy. But by an inevitable law every victory in the struggle must have brought with it the corresponding penalty. To know that he loved was to

now that he might be without love, to know that he was
appy was to know that he might be miserable, to know
hat he lived was to know that he would die. Having
aised himself above the animals, he had to give up things
he animals possessed.

In the growth of man's self-consciousness we have to do
with a range of feelings both complicated in its history and
resenting as urgent a problem to-day as in any period of
he past. Mankind cannot have accepted the growing
burden without many misgivings and partial reversions to
bestial heedlessness; and in the swing forward and back
how many kinds of courage and cowardice, acceptance
nd refusal of life, must have been implicated. To-day
he problem has altered because at last it has been formu-
ated explicitly. We know what has been lost and de-
iderate a quasi-animal spontaneity; we know what has
been won and refuse to surrender the keenest self-con-
ciousness. The problem is to combine the largest possible
proportion of both ideals. Twentieth century amateurs of
avage art prove how living the problem is, even if they
hirk the full issue. They exhibit a legitimate craving for
an imperilled spontaneity while duping themselves with
he notion that by satisfying this craving they can satisfy
lso the more complicated wants of mankind. Anyhow
he earlier stages of an important, long, and still develop-
ng process may well be expected to supply material for
oblique expression in poetry.

It is all too easy to confuse the primal melancholy with
ome sort of escape feeling, womb-nostalgia or what not;
and it is of the first importance for criticism to keep them
eparate. For those who felt the burden of self-consciousness too heavy, thoughts of escape were the inevitable
onsequence, while those who accepted the burden cannot
have lacked some misgivings at least. In all poetry where
he problem enters there must needs be some nostalgia
present. It is where the melancholy is isolated from the
oy which initially engendered it that there is a vicious
nostalgia. The true joy-melancholy means full acceptance

51489

of the situation and courage not to go back on the prima
human commitment.

In feelings such as these lies the secret of why mucl
poetry, especially lyric, appeals so profoundly and s
inexplicably, it seems, to us. Virgil, a more primitiv
poet than Homer for all the generalisations about natura
and artificial epics, is full of them.

For instance, the last hundred lines of *The Aeneid* hav
a quality of terror that goes quite beyond the context
Here Virgil has emerged from the welter of genera
warfare and is confronted with the culminating fight, th
death of Turnus at the hands of Aeneas. He chooses th
supernatural mechanism of Jupiter's sending a Fury t
baffle Turnus in the fight, and from the moment h
describes this bird of hell till the end of the poem he is a
the height of his powers. After the Fury has reached th
earth, she takes the form of a little bird that men hear cry
ing on tombs or lonely roof-tops, and flies backwards an
forwards shrieking in front of Turnus's face. Turnus'
limbs melt in terror:

> Postquam acies videt Iliacas atque agmina Turni,
> alitis in parvae subitam collecta figuram,
> quae quondam in bustis aut culminibus desertis
> nocte sedens serum canit importuna per umbras,
> hanc versa in faciem Turni se pestis ob ora
> fertque refertque sonans, clipeumque everberat alis.
> Olli membra novus solvit formidine torpor.[1]

This idea of compressing the great Fury into the littl
bird crying round the tombs is one of the most terrifyin
in literature; it cuts through all the comforting assurance

[1] 'When she espies the Ilian ranks and Turnus's columns, suddenl
shrinking to the shape of a small bird that often sits late by night o
tombs or ruinous roofs, and vexes the darkness with her cry, in suc
change of likeness the monster shrilly passes and repasses befor
Turnus's face, and her wings beat restlessly on his shield. A strang
numbing terror unnerves his limbs.'

ɔf civilised life. And when Turnus, face to face with
Aeneas, answers his threats with

> non me tua fervida terrent
> dicta, ferox: di me terrent et Iuppiter hostis

he is not Turnus speaking of the Latin pantheon, but man
confronted with the terrors of a hostile and inexplicable
universe.

Much of the melancholy in folk-music and ballads
may owe its power to its primitive quality. Take the
French nursery-rhyme 'Nous n'irons plus au bois.'
Although meant to accompany a children's dance, it is
charged with melancholy, especially in the first line.
The last verse sinks back into a normal acceptance of life.

> Nous n'irons plus au bois: les lauriers sont coupés.
> La belle que voilà, la lairons-nous danser!
> > Entrez dans la danse,
> > Voyez comme on danse.
> > > Sautez, dansez,
> > Embrassez qui vous voudrez.
>
> La belle que voilà, la lairons-nous danser!
> Mais les lauriers du bois, les lairons-nous faner?
>
> Mais les lauriers du bois, les lairons-nous faner?
> Non, chacune à son tour ira les ramasser.
>
> > * * *
>
> Cigale, ma cigale, allons, il faut chanter,
> Car les lauriers du bois sont déjà repoussés.
> > Entrez dans la danse,
> > Voyez comme on danse.
> > > Sautez, dansez,
> > Embrassez qui vous voudrez.

The powerful craving for such simple art-forms shows how
fundamental primitive feeling still is in ourselves and how
urgently it demands an outlet. When folk-literature was

common property, this craving was pretty well satisfied
and the primitive joys and fears do not find their way very
frequently into polite literature. There is little in Chaucer
for instance. It is significant, however, that when Shake
speare crowds his widest range of feeling into *Lear* the folk
song comes into its own as an organic part of the play. By
the eighteenth century, folk-literature had dropped out of
the range of life accepted by the educated classes without
any substitutes being provided. The consequent starva
tion partly accounts for the violence of the Romantic
Revival. In this heterogeneous period it is difficult to
sort out the healthy melancholy from the weak or morbid
nostalgia. In Lamartine the true melancholy is watered
down to a nostalgic weakness. Opinion differs on the
emotional sincerity of these lines of Shelley, but they may
be to the point here:

> Rough wind, that moanest loud
> Grief too sad for song;
> Wild wind, when sullen cloud
> Knells all the night long;
> Sad storm, whose tears are vain,
> Bare wood, whose branches strain,
> Deep caves and dreary main,—
> Wail, for the world's wrong.

The world's wrong: the evils of mankind in history
tyrannised over by priests and kings? Shelley may have
thought so; but actually he may be expressing the prima
melancholy of the human self-consciousness. And in the
succeeding periods it cannot but reappear. In our own
day, in spite of his protest at the opening of *The Dry
Salvages* that he does not know much about gods, T. S.
Eliot touches our sense of the primitive with conspicuou
success. In one place, even, he comes near to direc
statement:

> Between the idea
> And the reality

PRELIMINARY

Between the motion
And the act
Falls the Shadow
> *For Thine is the Kingdom*

Between the conception
And the creation
Between the emotion
And the response
Falls the Shadow
> *Life is very long*

Between the desire
And the spasm
Between the potency
And the existence
Between the essence
And the descent
Falls the Shadow
> *For Thine is the Kingdom.*

With the beasts no shadow falls between the motion and the act. With man's self-consciousness it is another matter.

The importance to mankind of expressing, of airing these primal feelings is great. Poetical obliquity is one of the chief instruments of this process.

In so obscure a region as that of the primitive it is most unlikely that the examples given will be generally accepted as apt. Yet the idea that there must be examples, that poetry is likely to preserve antique ways of feeling, accords perfectly with common sense and should command wide assent. And if poetry does this, it will seldom do so by methods other than the oblique.

2. SOME MEANS OF OBLIQUITY

(i) Preliminary

In this section, more than in any other, there occurs a difficulty that besets a book of this kind: the habit of the

examples' overlapping. In order to get some shape one
has to classify the means of obliquity under certain
features, such as symbolism, structure, or allusion. But
many of the examples defy a simple classification, exhibiting simultaneously and in equal degrees more than one of
these means. Here is a single example to illustrate the
difficulty: one of Catullus's poems to Lesbia. Before
getting to the point (that is, showing that Catullus uses
several of the means of obliquity) I shall have to spend
some words in talking of the poem generally and in showing that it is oblique and not direct.

> Vivamus, mea Lesbia, atque amemus,
> rumoresque senum severiorum
> omnes unius aestimemus assis.
> Soles occidere et redire possunt:
> nobis cum semel occidit brevis lux,
> nox est perpetua una dormienda.
> Da mi basia mille, deinde centum,
> dein mille altera, dein secunda centum,
> deinde usque altera mille, deinde centum.
> Dein, cum milia multa fecerimus,
> conturbabimus illa, ne sciamus,
> aut ne quis malus invidere possit,
> cum tantum sciat esse basiorum.[1]

On the face of it this is very direct statement indeed. It is
a practical incitement to defy convention, to make the
most of short life, to get on with the business of kissing.
Even if kissing stands for all or any acts of love, that is no
great obliquity; and if the number of kisses is hyperbolical,

[1] 'Let us live, my Lesbia, and let us love. And as for the murmur-
ings of crabbed old men let us value them at one penny. Suns may set
and return: for *us*, when once our brief light has set, there is one unbroken night to be slept out. Give me a thousand kisses, then a
hundred, then another thousand and a second hundred, then yet
another thousand, then a hundred. Then, when we have made up
many thousands, we will muddle the account, so that we may not
know it, and no envious person may be able to cast an evil spell on it,
when he knows that our kisses come to such a great sum.'

does this amount to more than reinforced statement? Of Catullus's fervour there can be no doubt, but does the fervour go beyond the practical issues stated? It does, because the formal features of the poem are in direct contrast to the single-hearted fervour of the sentiment. For all his heat of passion Catullus shows an uncommon intellectual coolness. *All* the old men's murmurs are valued at exactly *one* penny (that is why he puts *omnes* and *unius* side by side). His and Lesbia's mortality is not enough by itself, he must contrast it with the sun's perpetual rejuvenation. And the kissing is done in the regular sequence of a thousand followed by a hundred: they are not too passionate to count. And if the poem ends, as it began, with love, the penultimate line echoes the second in referring to the malice of the world without. To muddle the kissing-audit is an infantile game, typical of the ways of lovers. But there is no suspicion either that Catullus does not play it with abandonment or that he is not entirely aware how infantile it is. Passionate though the rhythm may be, it is rigorously confined and intensely sophisticated. Catullus succeeds in being at once Romeo and Baudelaire. Such a union makes the poem rich enough, and if the obliquity were confined to sophistication, it would be reasonable to use the poem as an example of obliquity through rhythm; for on the whole the rhythm is the main agent of giving this sense. But there is another, and perhaps more important obliquity that upsets this preponderance. So far, no more than a personal passion and a personal sophistication has been detected. Yet the poem is animated by a general idea. 'Let us live, my Lesbia, and let us love,' he begins; and by this simple exhortation he means life and love are one, love is the only life, life without love is death. The idea may be narrow and perverted; but enough people have felt it to make it important. And who has both felt and expressed it like Catullus? For the expression is the most truly poetical: the remotest possible from abstract thought. He quite simply isolates living and loving from all else; and by so doing identifies them. But he *says* nothing about their identity. Lastly, the very structure of the first line bears an oblique meaning. *Lesbia* is in the middle, enclosed by two unemphatic words, *mea* and *atque*, which are finally bounded by two very emphatic words *Vivamus* and *amemus*. Living and loving are not merely balanced or identified : they both revolve round Lesbia. Remove this centre and they both collapse.

The poem therefore is the oblique statement of an idea, of a lesser commonplace, and it uses both rhythm and structure as the means of obliquity. Nor does it tend towards any one of those headings sufficiently to make classification profitable.

(ii) Rhythm

I use the word 'rhythm' in a very wide sense : to cover all the effects that the sound of the words commands. Of course the range of effect commanded by pure sound apart from sense was greatly exaggerated in the late nineteenth century ; but it is likely that some moderns have gone too far in the other direction. Granted a minimum of sense to co-operate with sound, to get the reader's mind on the right road, sound can work very powerfully ; and rhythm is one of the major means of obliquity. The subject would be enormous if it were possible to say much about any large proportion of the many instances that offer themselves. But luckily or unluckily, it is exceedingly difficult to put into words our ideas about the verse whose main meaning is a rhythmic obliquity.

Rhythm is oblique when it does more than back up the professed sense, whether in backing up it quite overwhelms that sense yet without denying it, or whether it suggests something entirely alien or irrelevant. We get the largest bulk of this second kind when a very rigid convention dominates the lyric ; and the obvious example is the Petrarchising mode that invaded western Europe in the sixteenth century. Here it is only a small proportion of the output that has more than a nominal or cursory reference to its professed subject of adoring love. What this poetry really concerns remains a problem. Out of many possible examples of rhythmic obliquity in the Petrarchian convention take the following short poem of Wyatt:

> If in the world there be more woe
> Than I have in my heart,
> Whereso it is, it doth come fro [1],
> And in my breast there doth it grow
> For to increase my smart.   5
> Alas, I am receipt of every care,
> And of my life each sorrow claims his part.
> Who list to live in quietness
> By me let him beware,
> For I by high disdain   10
> Am made without redress,
> And unkindness, alas, hath slain
> My poor true heart all comfortless.

The true import of the poem has little to do with the serious condition the poet professes himself to be in. Like Donne in *A Nocturnal on St. Lucy's Day*, Wyatt professes himself the receptacle of every care the earth breeds. But the rhythm (unlike that of Donne's poem) does nothing to confirm this desperate situation; which is a mere polite fiction. The language is simple, and the collocation of words is not at all striking. Yet, though it has not the seriousness that fits the subject, the rhythm has a very marked seriousness of its own; and it is surprisingly varied. For instance, the line

> If in the world there be more woe

suggests a storminess of feeling absent from

> Alas, I am receipt of every care.

One has to speak the first line with vigour, the other falls easily though listlessly from the tongue. There is a suggestion of sing-song in lines 9 and 10. The monosyllables

---

[1] Fro=forth.

of the last lines must be pronounced with soft but distinct emphasis; they are very carefully controlled. To what do these varied rhythmic qualities point? Probably to one of the commoner subjects of obliquity, sensibility. They reveal a mind of acute but very healthily varied sensibility; a mind prone to outbursts of passion yet strongly controlled. The variety of rhythm suggests the elasticity of feeling; the rhythmic progress from storminess to control, those same qualities of the poet's mind. Experience proves how thoroughly the rhythm *is* the poem. Unread for some time, the poem fades from the mind; there are no arresting conjunctions of words to fix it. Yet as the rhythms are re-experienced, as they grow into the mind, the poem takes form surprisingly and cannot possibly be dismissed as trivial or lacking in substance. But the danger of dismissing such poems is considerable, for even though readers would not take Wyatt's Petrarchisings with full positive seriousness, they might easily take them seriously enough to prevent a sufficiently exclusive attention to the rhythm. To apply any but fully oblique standards to the poem is to misunderstand it. Judged by the standards of 'The glories of our blood and state' it is a total failure.

An example of how rhythm can of itself carry the reader into regions far beyond those of the professed subject is to be found at the end of the fifth book of *The Aeneid*. Here Virgil recounts how Palinurus, the steersman, is overcome by the god of sleep and falls overboard. The episode serves to contrast with the previous more vigorous narrative of the games and to lead up to the supernatural glories of Aeneas's descent to the underworld. It ends with the lines, spoken by Aeneas when he has discovered his ship drifting without a helmsman:

> O nimium caelo et pelago confise sereno,
> nudus in ignota, Palinure, iacebis harena.[1]

---

[1] 'Ah too trustful in calm skies and seas, thou shalt lie, O Palinurus, naked on an unknown sand.'

In the second line the meaning is not confined to the mere
sense of the words: to the pathetic contrast between
Palinurus's frivolous confidence in a clear sky and his
wretched fate. The sound of the line takes us away from
mere human accident to some more obscure experience.
Perhaps the 'unknown sand' is not so much the waste
place where Palinurus's naked body is to lie as the terrify-
ing wilderness that pressed against the borders of primitive
man's familiar haunts:

> What might this be? A thousand fantasies
> Begin to throng into my memory
> Of calling shapes, and beckning shadows dire,
> And airy tongues, that syllable mens names
> On Sands, and Shoars, and desert Wildernesses.

Anyhow, it is the halting, solemn rhythm that does most to
enrich the passage.

A poem in which Shelley very deliberately exploits a
shift in rhythm is the *Hymn of Pan*. Pan is here imagined
as singing at the contest between himself and Apollo before
Tmolus, the god of Mount Tmolus in Lydia. He sings of
his own skill in singing, of the audience of Sileni and
Nymphs he can attract and of the songs he has sung them;
and he ends:

> I sang of the dancing stars,
>   I sang of the daedal Earth,
> And of Heaven—and the giant wars,
>   And Love, and Death, and Birth,—
>   And then I changed my pipings,—
> Singing how down the vale of Maenalus
>   I pursued a maiden and clasped a reed.
> Gods and men, we are all deluded thus!
>   It breaks in our bosom and then we bleed:
> All wept, as I think both ye now would,
> If envy or age had not frozen your blood,
>   At the sorrow of my sweet pipings.

(*Ye*, in the antepenultimate line, are Apollo and Tmolus; and, in the penultimate, *envy* refers to Apollo, *age* to Tmolus.) Technically, the change of rhythm is simple enough. Shelley substitutes an iambic pentameter ('Singing how down the vale of Maenalus') for the ana-paestic trimeter expected on the analogy of the previous verses ('The wind in the reeds and the rushes'). But the break is completely effective, and the rest of the stanza, though metrically equivalent to what has gone before, has its tone quite transformed by the single irregular line. Rhythmically the change from joy to melancholy is effective. But how much does it effect, and does it do more than reinforce the statement? Have we an obliquity? Nominally the subject changes from nature and heroic subjects to disappointed love. Syrinx refused Pan's advances and was changed into a reed, which when clasped wounded his bosom. But the love-theme is slightly indicated; it has nothing in common with the heavily charged love-poetry of 'I fear thy kisses' or *The Indian Serenade*. The delusions to which gods and men are subject are not confined to love. It is a more general melancholy that that is meant. For the rhythmic sadness is no passing shudder of wind over the placid pool; it is complete and fundamental, though not stated with the full solemnity which Shelley at other times commanded.

(iii) Symbolism

I use the word *symbolism* in a narrow sense; for if it is allowed to spread out it includes too much to be of any service in this context. Yeats's two essays on symbolism in *Ideas of Good and Evil* are fine pieces of writing, but by the time he has finished with the word he has made it stand for most of the elements in art other than the purely informative:

> All Art that is not mere story-telling, or mere portraiture, is symbolic, and has the purpose of those symbolic talismans which mediaeval magicians made with complex colours and

forms, and bade their patients ponder over daily, and guard with holy secrecy; for it entangles, in complex colours and forms, a part of the Divine Essence.

Again, he calls 'symbolical' two lines of Burns which it hardly seems necessary to call anything more than normally poetical:

> There are no lines with more melancholy beauty than these by Burns—

> The white moon is setting behind the white wave,
> And Time is setting with me, O!

and these lines are perfectly symbolical. Take from them the whiteness of the moon and of the wave, whose relation to the setting of Time is too subtle for the intellect, and you take from them their beauty. But, when all are together, moon and wave and whiteness and setting Time and the last melancholy cry, they evoke an emotion which cannot be evoked by any other arrangement of colours and sounds and forms.

Now all the best poetry should work in the way Yeats here describes; all the parts should be organic: and to extend the word *symbolism* to cover so general a method is to make nebulous a word that might be handy if used more narrowly.

Symbolism, as I here use it, implies the use of certain objects as fixedly significant objects, not adjectivally sub-servient to other objects. It also implies the author's deliberate intention to give a symbolic meaning. The two lines of Burns would not fall within the category. The 'white moon' has but a passing function in the context, and there is no intention of deliberately equating it with any idea or system of ideas. It is more than physical moon; but its 'moreness' is not from within itself, it depends on all the other features of the two lines. On the other hand, Blake's rose in 'O Rose, thou art sick,' although it co-operates with the other parts of the poem, does, when the poem has been read, stand *by itself* for an idea. Blake called his poem *The Sick Rose*; and not for nothing: for though the sick rose in isolation is not the poem, and though the whole poem is needed for the data by which to isolate the rose correctly, the sick rose *by itself* has a significance that Burns's 'white moon' by itself has not.

Now it is precisely this isolation that gives symbolism one of its peculiar functions. But before enlarging on this I had better quote Blake's poem to serve as a general example of symbolism in poetry:

> O Rose, thou art sick!
> The invisible worm
> That flies in the night,
> In the howling storm,
>
> Has found out thy bed
> Of crimson joy,
> And his dark secret love
> Does thy life destroy.

Occurring as this poem does in *Songs of Experience*, it reveals its meaning easily. The rose is earthly love (with its potentialities of innocent fulfilment), the worm is the wicked instinct to be possessive and predatory that battens on and corrupts earthly love. (Let me say here, in order not to interrupt the argument later, that this poem is truly oblique. The comparison of corrupt love to a sick rose goes altogether beyond allegory or embroidered statement. The nature of the comparison is in itself more than the idea that love may be corrupted by possessiveness; it contains most of the meaning.) But quite apart from its context in *Songs of Experience*, the poem at once declares its symbolic nature. The first line violently personifies the flower, forces the mind to seek something more than the mere physical rose, and in so doing to dwell in surprise and curiosity on this sick flower. And the rest of the poem, though it may solve the puzzle, fixes the attention even more firmly on the place where it was first directed. For though the rose is clearly a symbol, Blake vivifies it by keeping the physical existence of the rose in our imaginations. Though in the first line he makes us know that his rose is more than a rose, he expresses in 'thy bed of crimson joy' the shape and the feel and the glow of the physical flower with incomparable felicity. The same phrase helps out the symbolic meaning, for it not only describes the physical rose but refers to the bed where the joys of love are experienced. The trend of the poem then is to make us dwell on the sick rose as the symbol of innocent love corrupted and see the sick rose as the sum of the poem.

Now, though the effect of such symbolism is apparently to narrow the mind to a couple of words, the actual effect is to encourage it to expand. The associations of any single word are limitless: directly it is set in a large context it is minutely narrowed. Similarly the symbol, of its very nature rising out of rather than mingling with its context, encourages an expansion of thought and association. In Blake's poem we are prone to follow out all the analogies between the rose and love, such as the bloom on the petals suggesting the bloom on a girl's cheek, in a way which would be quite illegitimate in reading the two lines of Burns.

When a great triumph of symbolism has been gained, as in Bunyan's Slough of Despond or Vanity Fair, it may be well for the author to leave it to take care of itself. Posterity will look after it. But symbolic detail is most effective through repetition. And anyhow, once a poet has gone to the trouble of creating a true symbol, something that has a permanent reference to a set of ideas, it is an obvious economy to repeat it. When the symbol has been established, the mere naming of it will present obliquely the whole body of associations it has collected. Moreover, by repetition you mitigate the dangers of over-expansiveness; for every fresh context limits *some* of the possible vagaries to which the isolated symbol might lead. How effective the repeated symbol could be we may realise if we imagine Blake's making the best use of his early successes. Having established certain admirable symbols in *Songs of Innocence and Experience*, like the lamb, the tiger, the rose, the watery shore, he throws away the enormous advantages of being able to use them again and painfully labours to create afresh a symbolism that lacks all the initial advantages of his previous creations. The normal mind leaps to greet Blake's tiger, it is persuaded to accept with strong approval his rose, and it can see some sense in the notion of making the watery shore signify the margin between material and eternal. With Los and Enitharmon it has to start at scratch, and is discouraged at the steeplechase it is expected to run.

In recent years Yeats and Eliot have used the recurrent symbol with great effect. Eliot has risked a great deal more on it than Yeats. In the later Yeats the symbols are mainly incidental. He uses them as suits him, and he can afford to drop them. 'Byzantium' is the symbol of passionless, eternal intellect in two poems; it does not spread through all his later volumes. In Eliot the symbols run through most of his verse. A successful symbol is used in this passage from the last section of *Ash-Wednesday*:

Although I do not hope to turn again
Although I do not hope
Although I do not hope to turn

Wavering between the profit and the loss
In this brief transit where the dreams cross
The dreamcrossed twilight between birth and dying
(Bless me father) though I do not wish to wish these things
From the wide window towards the granite shore
The white sails still fly seaward, seaward flying
Unbroken wings

'Profit and loss' sends the mind back to the lovely fourth section of *The Waste Land* where

Phlebas the Phoenician, a fortnight dead,
Forgot the cry of gulls, and the deep sea swell
And the profit and loss.

It prepares us for the mention of the sea, connected in *The Waste Land* with Tristan's voyage from Ireland, and symbolising the bravery of youthful passion. By no other means could the tug of earthly delight, the 'terrestrial stress,' be made to break more dazzlingly or more economically through the religious asceticism of *Ash-Wednesday* than by this recurrent sea-symbol. There are reasons why symbolism should suit Eliot's needs peculiarly well. It makes for structural tightness and gives the illusion of fixity, thus fulfilling Eliot's aspirations after 'classicism,' and it provides an outlet for that desire to expand which, for all his repudiation of the Romantic tradition, he has inherited from it.

Any very wide use of the fixed symbol in poetry is not likely to succeed. It is peculiarly liable to abuse. Excessively easy to invent, the fixed symbol risks becoming aridly mechanical on the one hand and fraudulently suggestive on the other. But capable as it is of powerful effect when used with economy it will always be valuable as a minor means of poetical obliquity.

(iv) Allusion

By *allusion* I mean a reference, conscious or unconscious, to a passage in literature. Allusion, like symbolism, is a minor obliquity. Its main function is to thicken the meaning of certain details. The obliquity consists in a statement's implying more than its words state because those words provoke a reference to a literary context, and that context, if known to the reader, cannot but supply an additional significance.

Much allusion is unconscious, but it should not on that account pass unnoticed. A poet might welcome the obliquity which his creating brain fashioned too quickly for his conscious mind to follow. Of such unconscious allusions there must be a vast number; many too faint even to be detected; many apparent to but a proportion of readers. Poets have their memories stored with the

works of other poets, and inevitably they will reproduce,
even if they modify, the rhythms that most fascinate them.
The following is a typical example of unconscious allusion
that it is worth becoming conscious of; it is typical also
because many readers might refuse to admit it altogether.
Yeats begins his *Sailing to Byzantium* as follows:

> That is no country for old men.   The young
> In one another's arms, birds in the trees,
> —Those dying generations—at their song. . . .

Here Yeats is probably referring to Keats's *Ode to a
Nightingale*:

> Thou wast not born for death, immortal Bird!
> No hungry generations tread thee down.

This unconscious reference enriches Yeats's lines.   If
Keats dwells on human mortality he does so because he
lives so intensely.   It is this intensity of living from which
in Yeats the escape is made to Byzantium and its 'monu-
ments of unageing intellect.'   The reference is a true
obliquity; it implies without a word of statement: and
the result is economy of space and enrichment of texture.

With this caution against treating allusion too simply, I
can go on to discuss what allusion means, of what it is the
oblique expression.   When plagiarism was very frequent
and people made use of a common stock of phrases,
allusion had no meaning at all.   Indeed it is hardly fair to
employ the word of such a state of things.   Allusion com-
plicates and is remote from the simple repetitions in ballad
literature.   In the ballads there is so much repetition that
the ultimate source of allusion is lost; the debt can no
longer be traced and perforce lapses.   Allusion means
some sort of fixity; and it begins when there exists a body
of classical literature known to everyone.   Before such a
time allusions will be mythological rather than literary.
In Greek literature allusion early became possible.   *The
Iliad* is felt as a permanent background to *The Odyssey*.
Aeschylus took the status of a classic writer with great

speed and offered allusive scope to his two successors.
Euripides, for instance, uses allusion to imply with what
pointed sophistication he is treating the legends in his
Electra. A very old attendant, clearly intended to belong
to an antiquated generation, brings Electra word that an
unknown man has laid offerings at Agamemnon's tomb:
could it be Orestes? When he suggests that Electra might
solve the question by comparing her feet with the unknown man's footprints, Euripides means us to think of
the *Choephoroe*, where such a comparison was the means of
identifying Orestes. Electra with stern common sense
reminds the enthusiastic old man that a brother's foot is
bigger than a sister's. By the allusion Euripides obliquely
conveys the information that he is deliberately treating
the legends in a different way from Aeschylus.

When once a tradition has been powerfully established,
allusion takes on a wide general function. Writers allude,
not always with any notion of specific relevance, but in
order to proclaim that they are fully aware of the tradition. Allusion then is an oblique statement of 'I am writing in the tradition, I am civilised, I know what I am
about, I am in touch with a civilised audience whom I can
count on to understand me.' Such allusion is most
frequent in the tradition of the classical epic. Many
allusions that appear at first sight to be worked in and are
condemned as frigidly academic may have this important
cultural significance. There is a quaint instance in the
ninth book of *Paradise Lost*. After Adam has shared the
forbidden fruit with Eve, the pair fall into lust, and Adam
ends his proposals with the lines

> For never did thy Beautie since the day
> I saw thee first and wedded thee, adorn'd
> With all perfections, so enflame my sense
> With ardour to enjoy thee, fairer now
> Than ever, bountie of this vertuous Tree.

Here Milton alludes to a passage in the fourteenth book of
The Iliad. Hera is in despair, because Zeus is allowing the

Trojans to win a battle, and has the idea of tempting him to love and sleep so that he may relax his sway. With the help of Aphrodite she succeeds, and Zeus as he yields to her says,

> οὐ γάρ πώ ποτέ μ' ὧδε θεᾶς ἔρος οὐδὲ γυναικὸς
> θυμὸν ἐνὶ στήθεσσι περιπροχυθεὶς ἐδάμασσεν ...
> ὡς σέο νῦν ἔραμαι καί με γλυκὺς ἵμερος αἱρεῖ.[1]

The analogy between the two contexts is not close. Homer writes in a comic, Milton in a tragic vein. Apart from the general analogy of female blandishment, to consider the two passages simultaneously would be to distort both. The main meaning of the allusion is something like this: 'I am writing my culminating book on the Fall; my subject is unusual: but I know what I am at; I am consciously in the great epic tradition.'

But Milton can make allusion mean more than that he is writing in the classical tradition. In the passage at the end of the *Second Georgic*, praising country life, Virgil thus protests his constant devotion to the Muses:

> Me vero primum dulces ante omnia Musae,
> quarum sacra fero ingenti percussus amore,
> accipiant.[2]

And Milton, after speaking of his blindness, alludes to this passage, in the following lines:

> Yet not the more
> Cease I to wander where the Muses haunt
> Cleer Spring, or shadie Grove, or Sunnie hill,
> Smit with the love of sacred song.

---

[1] 'For never did love of goddess or woman so overwhelm and tame the heart within my breast as the love and sweet desire for *you* that now seizes me.'

[2] 'Truly my first and foremost wish is that the sweet Muses (whose priest I am, struck with huge love) may receive me.'

ALLUSION

Percussus amore; smit with the love: there can be no doubt about the reference. And the effect is prodigious. Occurring, as both passages do, in contexts of the highest poetic intensity, they are like the two extremities of a flash of lightning, spots united by a blinding stream of electric fluid. In the common love of their art the two great poets as it were mingle their minds, each gaining sustenance from the other. In plainer prose, we feel Milton's context to be enriched through the reference and we trust Virgil's lines the more because they have animated the later poet.

All the above examples of allusion have this in common: that they refer to highly or reasonably familiar originals. Now it is dangerous to allude either to the too familiar or the too obscure. Very familiar passages tend to get isolated from their context and to become more a portion of speech than of literature. They get encrusted with stock associations and refuse to ramify as passages will when they are thought of in a very rich context. This is specially true of many biblical allusions. When allusion is obscure it tends to bear not the legitimate meaning of 'I acknowledge and accept the tradition,' but the less worthy one of 'I am of the small body of the elect.'

Apart from meaning 'I am traditional and proud of it,' or 'I am esoteric and proud of it,' allusion can of course mean any number of different things according to what it mentions and how it does so. But it does also encourage economy of words and concentration of much matter into a small space. In a minimum of words a large context rich in associations can be evoked. It thus works much in the manner of symbolism, and it is because of this concentration that both devices are much in vogue to-day. Its danger too is that of symbolism. It encourages the amateur to get big vague results too easily, to trade on the vast and vague evocative powers of great passages. In another way allusion is inappropriate to-day. The great age of allusion was the late seventeenth and early eighteenth centuries, when men were sincerely academic, when education was uniform and intensive, and when a sizeable audience could be

trusted to master a defined range of knowledge. In
Milton's day most of his readers would have had by heart
the whole passage from *The Georgics*. When they read
'smit with the love of sacred song,' they simply could not
miss the reference. To-day the state of things has changed,
and allusion cannot be more than a minor obliquity till
culture has once again become more standardised.

Still, it is true that allusion has been widely and successfully used in recent years, and I will illustrate by some
modern examples.

Like symbolism Eliot has used allusion with freedom
and elaboration, and with varied success. The opening of
The Waste Land will illustrate how great an economy allusion can effect without lapsing into over-vague evocation:

> April is the cruellest month, breeding
> Lilacs out of the dead land, mixing
> Memory and desire, stirring
> Dull roots with spring rain.
> Winter kept us warm, covering
> Earth in forgetful snow, feeding
> A little life with dried tubers.

That is his prelude, stating the anguished shrinking from
experience. But while we read we are meant to think of
another more famous prelude:

> Whan that Aprille with his shoures sote
> The droghte of Marche hath perced to the rote,
> And bathed every veyne in swich licour
> Of which vertu engendred is the flour. . . .
> Than longen folk to goon on pilgrimages.

There is the absolute contrast: the eager acceptance of
experience. The reference to Chaucer at once releases a
charge of feelings which by their contrast are entirely
appropriate to what Eliot has to say. Nor is there any
lack of tact: no sense of competing with Chaucer. The reference is so quiet: it may even have been unconscious.

ALLUSION

Eliot is not always so successful. His *Whispers of Immortality* is a poem in two contrasted halves. The first exhibits the sensuality of asceticism, the second the sensuality of the human flesh. It is slightly humorous, more than slightly horrible, and extremely solemn. The second half is adapted from *Carmen*, a poem in Gautier's *Emaux et Camées*. Here are Eliot's first and last verses:

> Grishkin is nice: her Russian eye
> Is underlined for emphasis;
> Uncorseted, her friendly bust
> Gives promise of pneumatic bliss.
>
> .   .   .   .
>
> And even the Abstract Entities
> Circumambulate her charm;
> But our lot crawls between dry ribs
> To keep our metaphysics warm.

And these are the two verses of *Carmen* that Eliot has copied:

> Carmen est maigre,—un trait de bistre
> Cerne son œil de gitana,
> Ses cheveux sont d'un noir sinistre,
> Sa peau, le diable la tanna.
>
> Les femmes disent qu'elle est laide,
> Mais tous les hommes en sont fous,
> Et l'archevêque de Tolède
> Chante la messe à ses genoux.

There are two objections to Eliot's allusion. First, it is relatively obscure. Many cultured English men and women have either not read Gautier at all, or have not remembered him well enough to get the reference. Secondly Gautier's banter is a damaging background for Eliot's solemnity. The Abstract Entities circumambulating Grishkin look elephantine when thought of along with the Archbishop's airy infatuation. Shades of Cotton

Mather and Emerson, that otherwise might have remained obscure, are inconveniently illumined by the play of Gallic sunshine.

Yeats uses allusion more sparingly but with great effect. This example comes from his *Two Songs from a Play* included in *The Tower*. The first of these songs sings of the two Dying Gods, Dionysus and Christ: Dionysus in the first verse, Christ in the second. Between these two oriental mystery-cults intervenes the rise of Rome ('another Troy') and Roman conquest ('another Argo'):

> Another Troy must rise and set,
> Another lineage feed the crow,
> Another Argo's painted prow
> Drive to a flashier bauble yet.
> The Roman Empire stood appalled:
> It dropped the reins of peace and war
> When that fierce virgin and her Star
> Out of the fabulous darkness called.

Although the rhyme-scheme is different, these lines refer to the last chorus in Shelley's *Hellas*:

> Another Athens shall arise

and

> A loftier Argo cleaves the main
> Fraught with a later prize.

The effect is tremendous. It is only when Yeats's fierce irony is set against the background of Shelley's most serene and passionate idealism that it gets its full force.

(v) Plot

The word *plot* can serve so many purposes that I had better explain my use of it. Originally a synonym for the *fable*, translating Aristotle's μῦθος, it meant the putting together of the incidents in a narrative or dramatic poem. It certainly could not, in its early use, have been applied to the construction of a lyric. To-day there is no violence in speaking of the way Marvell plotted *To his Coy Mistress*. In this chapter *plot* stands for any expressive juxtaposition or organisation, not only of incidents but of any literary features of similar nature. I said in the last section that Eliot's *Whispers of Immortality* was a poem in two contrasted halves, the first exhibiting the sensuality of asceticism, the second that of the human flesh. The plot of the poem consists in this juxtaposition, while any cross-references from one half to the other are subordinate portions of the plot. In an earlier chapter Catullus's line,

Vivamus, mea Lesbia, atque amemus,

was quoted as an example of plot-obliquity. Such an oblique method is found equally in the longest literary forms, prose as well as verse. Arnold Bennett's *Old Wives' Tale* is pre-eminent among his novels largely on account of its plot-obliquity. It tells the contrasted stories of Sophia and Constance Baines. Sophia elopes and has an exciting life in Paris, Constance remains in the Potteries and marries the chief assistant in the paternal shop. But however much Arnold Bennett excites us by describing the siege of Paris or an execution at Auxerre, he does so just as much when he shows us Mr. Povey dressing the shop-window, or Constance in her rheumatic old age heroically dragging herself out of doors to vote against an important municipal reform. By his juxtaposition Bennett conveys with much power his conviction that *all* life is wonderful. Thus *plot* may cover something as short as a line of Catullus and as long as *The Old Wives' Tale*.

To call plot the main potential obliquity is to please more readers now than twenty years ago. But even now most people are slow to grant it any large share of meaning. Plot is so often considered as no more than a necessary 'mechanic beauty'; something that the Victorians heeded too little, but something within the competence of any intelligent and industrious author. The reason for this is that much perfect plotting is ineffective, and that the virtue of the plot only begins when other qualities are already there. Many modern detective-stories are ephemeral in spite of excellent plotting. Some of Cowley's worst lyrics are faultlessly put together. But that does not mean that plot is never important. Easy though it is for a cool self-possessed mind to plot ingeniously, it becomes a matter of greater difficulty and greater importance when the imagination grows hot. The cool brain has no temptations not to plot well, but without these temptations plotting well amounts to nothing. Now, as the other capacities of an author expand, so does the plot grow in relative importance to those capacities. The power to keep control, to force all the parts into proportion, even in the very height of excitement, is the crowning act of poetic greatness.

In a general sense, then, plot signifies order and control: it is the chief means of giving the impression of what we loosely call *greatness*. But besides this it can have other less general meanings. First and most important, it is the commonest and most effective means of putting the great commonplaces obliquely. Out of the mere bringing together of the different sorrows of Priam and Achilles Homer extracts his commonplace that the things that unite mankind count for more than those that divide them. Such a juxtaposition would be useless, even ridiculous, without the qualities of human insight, closeness to actual life, rhythmic skill and so on that Homer commands; but co-existing with them it expresses most of all. Moreover it is totally oblique, giving its meaning without any trace of statement whatever.

Secondly, plot expresses most effectively the adaptable comprehensiveness of a fine mind. Plot is the largest but least obtrusive manifestation of wit (in the seventeenth century sense). One of the reasons why Marvell's *To his Coy Mistress* satisfies us so thoroughly is that the minor manifestations of wit gracefully subordinate themselves to the plot of the poem, to the major contrasts between the poem's three paragraphs. Shakespeare expresses his adaptable comprehensiveness by so many other means, such as rhythm, thought, and character, that it is easy to overlook the less obvious means of plot. Yet he does use it, and, when he does, with eminent effect. *Much Ado About Nothing* is witty in this way; and that because the verbal brilliance is subordinated to what the plot is after, and the plot is insinuating at every turn the unaccountable ironies of fortune to which the sensible mind will learn to adapt itself. 'Unless you keep a sense of proportion,' says the plot obliquely, 'life will make you ridiculous.' Claudio and Hero, two less important people than Benedick and Beatrice, are the chief figures of the main plot. Through a freak of fate their story nearly ends in tragedy, but not quite. They arouse unnecessary passions in other people, and all the pains that these folk take to clear up the trouble are futile because the fantastic incompetence of Dogberry and his fellows anticipates by a fluke the carefully directed efforts of their betters. 'What your wisdoms could not discover, these shallow fools have brought to light.' Beatrice, the potentially tragic figure, with a brilliant intellect, not only wastes her efforts in setting Benedick against Claudio, but has her love awakened by a trick that a less brilliant person might well have suspected. And, final irony, the trick itself was probably superfluous, because Benedick and Beatrice are deeply attracted to each other from the start and would have got married in any case. It is this plot-obliquity, complicated but directed to one end, that makes *Much Ado* one of Shakespeare's most satisfying comedies.

Within these three meanings, control, the great commonplaces, and wit, plot may of course express a multitude of notions, which it would be profitless to enumerate. I can best explain the richness of plot-obliquity through some examples.

Not only Marvell's *Coy Mistress* but his *Picture of Little T. C. in a Prospect of Flowers* works mainly through plot. This consists in an even, quiet, unsuspicious progression crossed by an incredibly sudden turn at the end. The

77

whole plot-obliquity springs from the single contrast. At the opening T. C. is presented to us practising her arts, which later will become so formidable, upon the flowers. With her fair aspect she tames the wilder ones, but, young aristocrat or prude as she is, plays with the roses alone. But as she tames the flowers, so later will her chaste scorn tame the wanton Cupid. Here the poet interposes a slight but not insignificant contrast. He must make his peace with this dangerous beauty before it is too late, before her eyes have grown to their mature power. 'Let me be laid,' he says, 'where I may see thy Glories from some shade.' He must get out of the full brilliance of their beams. Whither? *Laid* and *shade* suggest the grave initially, and though we reject this meaning in the context, we do not forget what we have rejected. Then we go back to the opening theme. Little T. C. may get on with the immediate business of teaching the flowers their lessons: with exquisite gravity she is told to 'reform the errors of the Spring.' Then in the last verse, just as we are successfully lulled by having been recalled to the beginning, the poet springs his surprise on us: the previous hint of death leaps up at us with a suddenness made the greater because this time the little girl herself, so unconscious of mortality, is the possible victim:

> But O young beauty of the Woods,
> Whom Nature courts with fruits and flow'rs,
> Gather the Flow'rs, but spare the Buds;
> Lest *Flora* angry at thy crime,
> To kill her Infants in their prime,
> Do quickly make th' Example Yours;
> And, ere we see,
> Nip in the blossome all our hopes and Thee.

Not that the plot gets its effect unaided; on the contrary, other parts must co-operate in order that plot may have its proper chance. For instance, the solemn but subdued vibrations of the line,

> Gather the Flow'rs, but spare the Buds,

coming after the languid movement of the previous stanza, have a rhythmic surprise that strongly reinforces the plot-obliquity. So too the elegant fictions of the first four stanzas are all necessary to create in the reader a state of mind unable to resist the major contrast when it comes. Granted the plot-obliquity, what does it mean? This vivid juxtaposition of budding life and blighting death certainly expresses forcefully such a commonplace as 'death haunts the sunniest day,' or the more reflective one 'we can only live well in the thought of life's brevity.' These were the thoughts of the age in which Marvell lived, and to express them with uncommon vividness in verse would be to make good poetry. But the obliquity means more; it gives us contact with a mind of uncommon richness. No poet in Marvell's day, except the Milton of *Lycidas*, could turn his mind so athletically from one pole of feeling to another, could be so alert in apprehending so many experiences simultaneously. Without being great, Marvell's mind was so well organised, it was so free from wastage, he made such finished use of what he possessed, that he satisfies us in a manner which many greater poets miss. To use a metaphor, his modest fire is pure anthracite, and gives a clearer glow than more prodigal blazes of 'cobbles' or 'nuts.'

Sir Arthur Quiller-Couch, in his lecture on *The Horatian Model in English Verse*, suggests the pleasing picture of Milton and Marvell experimenting upon the Horatian model during office hours when they were Civil Servants. There is no doubt that Marvell had studied Horace closely, and that he may have derived his love of the well-plotted lyric from the Roman poet. Certainly Horace, as A. Y. Campbell pointed out very well in his study, depends on plot and surprise to an extent uncommon in English verse; and my next example of plot-obliquity is his ode on the Bandusian spring:

> O fons Bandusiae, splendidior vitro,
> Dulci digne mero non sine floribus,

Cras donaberis haedo,
Cui frons turgida cornibus

Primis et Venerem et proelia destinat.
Frustra: nam gelidos inficiet tibi
Rubro sanguine rivos
Lascivi suboles gregis.

Te flagrantis atrox hora Caniculae
Nescit tangere, tu frigus amabile
Fessis vomere tauris
Praebes et pecori vago.

Fies nobilium tu quoque fontium,
Me dicente cavis impositam ilicem
Saxis, unde loquaces
Lymphae desiliunt tuae.[1]

It is a popular little poem, partly because it is easy to
construe and partly because it appeared to provide what
most nineteenth century readers looked on as pleasantly
and correctly poetic, a straightforward nature-poem.
Alas, they deceived themselves; for the poem is sophisticated and deals with nature in that subordinated way
which was usual with Horace and which caused him on
the whole to be so little loved in the Romantic epoch.
For the major meaning of the poem is the plot, and however fond Horace may have been of his fountain he puts
the unsuspecting thing very much to his own uses. The
poem is worked out as follows. The occasion, or the
supposed occasion, is the eve of the Fontanalia or feast of
fountains, when it was the custom to honour them with

[1] 'Spring of Bandusia, brighter than glass, worthy of sweet wine
and of flowers too, to-morrow shalt thou be offered a kid whose brow
swelling with his first horns foretells both love and battle. In vain, for
he shall stain thy cold wells with his red blood, child of a wanton
flock. Thou canst not be touched by the fierce season of the blazing
dog-star. Thou givest delicious coolness to the bulls weary from the
plough and to the wandering flock. Thou too shalt be numbered
among the famous springs, when I tell of the oak planted on those
hollow rocks, whence thy murmuring waters leap down.'

flowers and wine. Horace, admitting that Bandusia is worthy of the usual offering, states with considerable circumstance that he will honour it exceptionally with a sacrificial victim. And with a good one too, an animal on the threshold of age, ready for love and war, but still virgin. After this swift and pretentious climax the tone drops and remains rhythmically lowered till the end. Horace reverts to the agreeable qualities of the fountain; and then, just as the poem is trickling quietly out, and in a very unobtrusive and matter-of-fact manner, almost indeed as an afterthought, he imparts the surprising news that he is giving his fountain immortal fame:

Fies nobilium tu quoque fontium.

The plot then works out as follows: description, expected and conventional; climax, apparent and studiedly magnil-oquent, but a fake; more description suggesting the close; real climax, studiedly cool and understated. What, then, does the poem mean? Some sort of humorous awareness of the inconsequences and incongruities of life; the ridi-culousness of pomp to the discerning eye, the undramatic manner in which important events so often happen. That is the sort of meaning, issuing solely from the plot and of the purest obliquity, that quite overshadows the apprecia-tion of a natural beauty that certainly is not entirely absent from the poem.

I go on to longer poems whose crowning merit is what they achieve through plot-obliquity. And first *Lycidas*, which I mentioned at the opening of this book as a typical example of oblique poetry.

First, it may be assumed that readers have abandoned the simplicities of Johnson's criticism of *Lycidas*, and, although the nominal subject is an elegy on a friend, they will not be distressed if they find Milton's main meaning to be something different. Secondly, it is a useful pointer towards the possible mood of the poem to realise that Milton, having gone through a long spell of study for his life-work, was about to complete it by travelling to Italy

F

and Greece. He had written little, and he must have been increasingly anxious, as he proceeded in his preparations, lest any accident should prevent his carrying out the great plans on which he had decided to risk everything. Thirdly, in a poem of such richness, it is impossible to explain the plot-obliquity without speaking of the other, reinforcing, qualities.

Lycidas is plotted in six sections: four main sections with prologue and epilogue. The prologue, consisting of the first twenty-four lines, makes it clear that Milton is thinking of himself as much as of Edward King, for he speaks of his own possible death, his 'destin'd Urn' and 'sable shroud.' The first section, lines 25 to 84, expresses grief, regret, bafflement. Why should Lycidas have died? The nymphs should have saved him. Yet what could they do against the course of fate? Even the Muse, a goddess, could not save her son Orpheus. And the uncertainty of things fixes itself in his own case. Why take an infinity of pains when it may be all for nothing? A voice from heaven gives the answer. The reward is in heaven not on earth:

Of so much fame in Heav'n expect thy meed.

So ends the first section. But by some rhythmic subtlety Milton robs the heavenly protest of any convincingness. It is what *should* comfort him and yet it does not. As a whole the section expresses a sense of wrong in the order of things, not to be righted by the conventional comfort of a heavenly adjustment. The opening lines of the second section indicate that a prolonged pause precedes them:

O Fountain *Arethuse*, and thou honour'd flood,
Smooth-sliding *Mincius*, crown'd with vocall reeds,
That strain I heard was of a higher mood:

the poet listens, incredulous, to the voice from heaven and reverts to his sorrowful theme. As a whole the second section, lines 85 to 131, reinforces the uneasiness of the

first. It utters more violent passions, obstinate questionings, anger, fierce resentment at human fate and earthly
injustice. The corrupt clergy typify Milton's sense of the
wrongness of things, and this time no voice from heaven
interposes: on the contrary, Milton inserts the colossal
grimness of 'and nothing sed' and ends with his vague
prophecy of retribution. So far the development has been
fairly simple. The two sections have been like two waves,
the second larger than the first, but coming from the same
direction and breaking on the same shore. Milton has
stated his quarrel with the existing order of things, and we
expect some sort of solution or closing comment. Instead
we get one of the most enchanting mutations in poetry.
After the final ferocity of the 'two-handed engine' comes
the unruffled but intense gentleness of

> Return *Alpheus*, the dread voice is past,
> That shrunk thy streams; Return *Sicilian* Muse,
> And call the Vales, and bid them hither cast
> Their Bels, and Flourets of a thousand hues.

From bitter present actuality we are plunged in full
Arcadia and mythical romance. Nor is the change
irrelevant to the thought. Abrupt as it is, it proffers a
possible solution, that of escape; ignoble if it were final,
but as an interlude vastly extending the poem's range of
experience. But even in offering the solution Milton will
have none of it. He knows it is a false surmise with which
he dallies, and though he takes us with him in his romantic
quests, we await the true solution in the fourth section
(lines 165 to 185). Here Milton tells the shepherds to
weep no more for Lycidas, but under this guise he declares
his own awakened courage in face of the wrongs he feels so
acutely; the picture of heavenly beatitude fully answers
his obstinate questionings. In other words, the apotheosis
of Lycidas figures forth Milton's own reconcilement with
the difficulties of life. The obliquity of the epilogue is
mainly rhythmic. Poetically these eight lines have the
intense serenity of the last lines of the *Paradiso*. There is in

them the profoundest peace, not of lethargy but of impulses harmonised; the peace of utter conviction.

The plot of *Lycidas* does not mean, by itself, anything quite so plain as that of *O Fons Bandusiae*, but it largely contributes to express a very important commonplace and the sense of a very rich mind. *Lycidas* does indeed combine all the major meanings that plot can best command. Rigorously controlled for all the tumult of passion contained in the poem, the plot conveys better than any other feature a sense of power. The sudden plunge from bitter actuality to Arcadia, from contemporary politics to utter escape, reveals a mind both vastly capacious and exquisitely aware of different states of feeling. But out of the whole poem, not implied by the plot but as it were vouched for by the sense of greatness created by the plot, emerges one of the greatest commonplaces. The poem ends with the poet's resolution to go on with his proper work. He has overcome his inhibiting fears; he can face the risk of doing all for nothing, he can bear the sight of human injustice. So much the reader may grant; he may be less willing to grant the further commonplace into which the meaning of the poem seems to distil itself. And no wonder, for this meaning is so oblique, so unsupported by statement, that no proof is possible. But the central commonplace of the poem is a part of the Christian paradox, 'Whosoever will lose his life shall find it'; perhaps the statement 'Personal integrity is more important than anything.' Results do not matter, abandon them, lose your life: and you will find yourself. As well as being Christian it is the doctrine that Krishna taught Arjuna in the Bhagavadgita. It is through the emergence of this commonplace that *Lycidas* is altogether a greater poem than *Little T. C.* Marvell accepted sincerely the thought of his age. Milton took nothing for granted; he reached his commonplace through sheer personal experience; he lived it and all the unease that led to it, from the beginning; and he gave it new life by a perfect restatement. *Lycidas* is at once the greatest poetry and complete obliquity.

My last example of plot-obliquity is Chaucer's *Miller's Tale*. This is usually thought a brilliantly-told piece of bawdry, no more: coarse fun plus one of the familiar Chaucerian features, narrative power. Actually it is a consummate piece of obliquity, yet so elusive, so apt to turn another front to you when you read it again, that to explain the obliquity is tantalisingly difficult. And yet *not* to call it oblique at once lands you in worse trouble. Of all great English poets Chaucer is the most patently sane; but if he spent his best skill of plotting and character-drawing on mere pleasant 'harlotrye' he must have been temporarily mad. For it is the most brilliantly plotted of all the *Tales* and the character-sketches in no way yield to those of the Prologue. It is in the clear, economical style of Chaucer's maturity: the earlier padding or rambling have disappeared. What was he after that he should take so much trouble?

Chaucer will not tell us: although he created his own opportunity; for the Miller did not begin his tale without discussion. When the Knight had finished, the Host very reasonably asked the Monk, who of the pilgrims came next in social seniority, to have the next turn. But the Miller had grown unruly with ale and insisted on breaking in. The Host did not like to cross him and let him have his way. Chaucer interposes with his apology to the reader that the Miller *would* tell his tale and that he can take no responsibility for it:

> What sholde I more seyn, but this Millere
> He nolde his wordes for no man forbere,
> But tolde his cherles tale in his manere;
> Me thinketh that I shal reherce it here.
> And therfore every gentil wight I preye,
> For goddes love, demeth nat that I seye
> Of evel entente, but that I most reherce
> Hir tales alle, be they bettre or werse,
> Or elles falsen som of my matere.
> And therfore, who-so list it nat y-here,

Turne over the leef, and chese another tale;
For he shal finde y-nowe, grete and smale,
Of storial thing that toucheth gentillesse,
And eek moralitee and holinesse;
Blameth nat me if that ye chese amis.
The Miller is a cherl, ye knowe wel this;
So was the Reve, and othere many mo,
And harlotrye they tolden bothe two.
Avyseth yow and put me out of blame;
And eek men shal nat make ernest of game.

Is this no more than Chaucer's way of telling the reader to skip the bawdry if he likes? Hardly: the specious apology of the first lines, the pretence that he had to be true to what his characters narrated (when he need not have introduced low characters at all), is only the prelude to more speciousness. 'Let the squeamish reader turn the page and he will find virtuous matter enough; and don't let him blame *me* if he chooses amiss.' On the surface it means no more than that if the virtuous reader choose amiss (that is, to read a bawdy tale) it is not Chaucer's fault, because other fare has been provided. But ... *choose amiss* is ambiguous: it might mean one thing to the virtuous reader and to Chaucer another. It *could* mean, 'If you're such a fool as to skip what you, if you had any taste, could see after a few lines was going to be one of my best stories, blame your own foolish and prudish self, not *me* for having thrown dust in your eyes.' However, though Chaucer lets us know that he takes *The Miller's Tale* seriously, of what the seriousness is composed his prefatory lines give no hint.

Like *Little T. C.*, *The Miller's Tale* gets its supreme effect by a single stroke of plot, and gives us warrant for that effect by the excellence both of subordinate plot-features and of other parts of the poem. Indeed these other features are so good that, as in *Lycidas*, it is impossible to isolate the obliquity into plot alone. We have to do with the complicated obliquity of great poetry. I shall have to go to some length to substantiate this.

The story opens with the description of Nicholas, an Oxford undergraduate, who has lodgings with John, a well-to-do but stupid carpenter. Thirty lines of Chaucer's innocent-sounding verse fix the man's character for good and show us that we are reading a careful work of art. Nicholas was a 'poor scholar,' but nevertheless he had an elegant room to himself (unlike most poor scholars). He looked like a girl and scented himself. His hobbies were astrology, through which he was particularly good at foretelling the weather, and music. His favourite song was *Angelus ad Virginem*, an actual Annunciation hymn: but, when we remember that with his girlish appearance he looked something like an angel himself, we suspect a further meaning in his song's title. (Throughout the poem there is a delicate mixing of the sacred and the obscene.) The last two lines of the description are the purest honey of Chaucer's irony:

> And thus this swete clerk his tyme spente
> After his freendes finding and his rente.

In other words, this sly and idle undergraduate wastes his time with a thoroughness that fluctuates with his own income and his friends' subsidies.

The first piece of plotting is to put, without a word of comment, a short description of the carpenter alongside that of Nicholas. In twelve lines Chaucer shows us, self-doomed and star-crossed, the comic victim, elaborates his irony, and gives us the one possible hint of what the oblique features of his story may mean:

> This Carpenter had wedded newe a wyf
> Which that he lovede more than his lyf;
> Of eightetene yeer she was of age.
> Ialous he was, and heeld her narwe in cage,
> For she was wilde and yong, and he was old,
> And demed himself ben lyk a cokewold.
> He knew nat Catoun, for his wit was rude,
> That badde man sholde wedde his similitude.

Men sholde wedden after hir estaat,
For youthe and elde is often at debaat.
But sith that he was fallen in the snare,
He moste endure, as other folk, his care.

To bring the carpenter and 'Catoun' together is exquisitely ludicrous : and the couplet in which Chaucer does so is tight packed with implications. The gravity with which he suggests that if the carpenter had had the advantages of reading Cato he might have avoided his error is perfect comedy; and radiating from it are the ironic propositions that the working classes ought to read Cato and the like, because these are the only means of access to the mother-wit which is the common heritage of the folk, and that those who have read Cato never by any chance fall into the carpenter's error. Further, Chaucer insinuates, 'I know I am a book-worm and adore theoretical wisdom, but I laugh at myself for it,' and 'I hope that some of my readers may not know that I am laughing at myself but may make fools of themselves by thinking themselves wiser than I am and calling me obtuse and academic.' The last two lines give clearly and briefly the comic setting. They place the victim in the light of remorseless reason, but they do not isolate him from society. He is like other sinners against the wisdom of the race; not like the tragic victim, erring but mysteriously singled out by Fate for special suffering. We have to do with the way of the world, not the ways of God.

Sandwiching the carpenter ruthlessly between the 'swete clerk' and her fragrant self, Alison is next described. She is a brilliant study in black and white, and her wanton eye, black as a sloe, under her plucked eyebrows, settles the elderly husband's fate more firmly than ever. Then the action begins. The carpenter has work at the Abbey of Osney, and is sometimes absent. Nicholas and Alison soon arrange to go to bed together at the first convenient opportunity. The arrangement made, 'this gode wyf,'

Chaucer tells us, went on a saint's day to church,

Christes owne werkes for to wirche,

with her forehead shining as bright as day; and her piety
introduces us to the fourth character, the flamboyant
Absolon, a 'parish-clerk.' His curly gold hair, which stuck
out like a fan, his red complexion and grey eyes, his red
and blue clothes, contrast with the hard black and white
in Alison's picture. And in character this merry and
versatile man, who made music in all the taverns, is very
different from the secretive Nicholas. There is in fact an
elaborate plot-contrast between the characters. Absolon,
who enjoys his duty of censing the wives, is smitten with
Alison. Instead of working secretly and swiftly, he
serenades her and pesters her with presents. He even
plays Herod in a Miracle Play to attract her attention.
Alison prefers the man on the spot.

Then follows the main intrigue. The carpenter,
credulous of Nicholas's weather-wisdom, is persuaded that
the stars foretell a second flood next Monday; he must
hang three great kneading-troughs from the roof-beams
for Alison, Nicholas, and himself, with provisions and an
axe each for cutting loose when the water comes. Farcical
in itself, Chaucer keeps the plot to comedy by the brilliant
pictures of domestic life the story unfolds: the man-
servant peeping through the hole made for the cat into
Nicholas's room and seeing Nicholas feigning a swoon with
gaping mouth and goggle eyes; servant and master priz-
ing open the door. Moreover the plot is tightly controlled.
After the three have climbed their newly-made ladders
into their tubs, the stupid carpenter, just because he was
dog-tired from all the work he had to do, falls into a dead
sleep, which he advertises by snoring, 'for his heed mislay.'
Nicholas and Alison climb down their ladders and proceed
to make the best use of their opportunity.

But there had been another consequence of the main
intrigue. The carpenter had stayed away from his work
at Osney. Now Absolon, happening to be at this place on

the Monday, makes discreet inquiries about the carpenter. He is told that perhaps the carpenter is away for a couple of days buying wood. Absolon thinks that now is his chance; and in the small hours of the morning begins serenading outside the window of the room where Nicholas and Alison are in bed together. Alison tells him to go away, but he persists, and our whole attention is then fixed on the ensuing farce: the carpenter snores remote from our attention. Absolon begs at least a kiss, and is granted one, but not of the kind he expected. Vowing revenge, and cured for good of his amorous imaginings, he borrows a hot iron from the blacksmith and returns for another kiss. This time Nicholas comes to the window, to get the hot iron clapped to his buttocks. And then the miracle happens, and the different pieces of the plot fly together; for Nicholas in his pain yells for water, the carpenter starts out of his sleep, hears the cry, thinks the Flood has come, and cutting the rope, crashes down on the floor beneath. The surprise, the sudden union of the two themes, is sublime. It is as if, for a fraction of a second, the heavens opened and we saw all the gods watching the trivial and ridiculous human comedy below.

The Miller's Tale is a coarse story. But though Chaucer enjoyed the coarseness, he made it strictly subserve the main ends of the plot; for it is the very outrageousness of the farce which, drawing the reader's mind away from the main plot, leaves it at the poet's disposal when he chooses to recall it.

Chaucer ends with the mathematical morality proper to comedy: the characters get what they have deserved:

> Thus swyved was the carpenteres wyf,
> For al his keping and his Ialousye;
> And Absolon hath kist her nether ye;
> And Nicholas is scalded in the toute.
> This tale is doon, and god save al the route!

What of Alison? Nothing is said of her reward, nor need it be. She had fulfilled her part of the equation beforehand by the anticipatory punishment of being married to a jealous old husband.

I have mentioned the main features of the poem: the great stroke of surprise through the plot, the exact, almost mathematical working out of the plot generally, the unerring characterisation, and the closeness to actual life. Taken together, what do they mean? Mathematical perfection of plot need mean very little. In that kind of perfection (apart from Chaucer's stroke of surprise) a play of Somerset Maugham is as well contrived as *The Miller's Tale*: yet it is hollow; the plot means little more than a high ingenuity. But in conjunction with the characterisation Chaucer's brilliant plot means a great deal. Comedy deals with individual caprice at variance with society; and society, implying a norm and limitations, must win in the end. These limitations can be expressed in more than one way. Restoration Comedy expresses them by the code of manners implied by what the characters say. Chaucer too expresses them, but far more obliquely, through the perfect orderliness of his plot, and also by the elegant economy of his language. Against this order his charming but offending victims are set, and they get their reward. Not that he judges them morally, but he shows them up against the normal background of what the world insists on being. Chaucer's extreme sensitiveness and sympathy extend the comic view of life to a very unusual range.

But the meaning of *The Miller's Tale* goes beyond the normally comic. How much significance the plot yields depends largely on how seriously the features other than plot are to be taken. Now Chaucer's characterisation should be taken very seriously indeed. However direct in appearance, it has an oblique meaning, and however objective, it has a psychological correlative in Chaucer's mind. The quality it most expresses is a strong, acute, and eager sensibility. Chaucer absorbed and was absorbed by the characters of those around him with vehemence: the kind of vehemence Keats showed towards pure sensation and D. H. Lawrence towards his birds, beasts, and flowers.

Supplemented by the sensibility, vouched for, as it were, by it, the plot of *The Miller's Tale* acquires an abstract significance analogous to that of good music or of the best Byzantine mosaics. And when Chaucer delivers his master-stroke, bringing back the carpenter into the story through Nicholas's yelling for water, he gets beyond the social bounds of comedy and impels the reader's mind to exult and to expand as it does in enjoying the very greatest art. From the side of comedy Chaucer loses himself in an *O Altitudo*; and feelings akin to those of religious wonder are the ultimate obliquity issuing from all the parts and especially from the plot of *The Miller's Tale*.

(vi) Character

The question of character has been complicated by an assumption that prevailed during the last century and is only now being seriously called in doubt. This assumption sprang from the paramount value given to sheer motivation, to psychological insight; and it was influenced by current notions of progress. Greek tragedy was considered as good as it could be in the circumstances, but compared with the Shakespearean there was something a little mechanical about it. With its insistence on Fate, it gave insufficient scope to the human being. Hence Aristotle's insistence on plot: mistaken but understandable. Had he known Shakespeare he would have judged otherwise. Compared with Orestes, Hamlet reveals far deeper profundities of soul. And it is assumed that this is a definite gain. By his prodigality of character-detail Shakespeare is more 'inward' than Aeschylus. But Shakespeare is only part way along the road of dramatic progress. There is much in him, especially the battle-scenes, that is crudely external; and though no dramatist has rivalled him in achievement, some may have improved on his method. Ibsen, for instance, shows the inward conflict more purely, as far as method goes, than Shakespeare, and hence is further forward on the road.

CHARACTER

I will illustrate the kind of critical error these assumptions led to, from two great poems. The *Prometheus Bound* of Aeschylus was not recognised for the very great literature it is till the Romantic epoch. But the generations of Ossian and of the French Revolution could hardly fail to notice the romantic setting of the play in the mountains of the Caucasus and the nobly revolutionary character of Prometheus. All the emphasis was put on those features. No wonder if Shelley chose this play to inspire the most elaborate pronouncement of his special creed, or if the inspiration was confined to the setting and the character of the protagonist. This from Shelley's preface to *Prometheus Unbound* shows how strongly he puts the emphasis on character. After comparing Aeschylus's Prometheus with Milton's Satan, Shelley writes:

> Prometheus is, in my judgment, a more poetical character than Satan, because, in addition to courage, and majesty, and firm and patient opposition to omnipotent force, he is susceptible of being described as exempt from the taints of ambition, envy, revenge, and a desire for personal aggrandisement, which, in the Hero of *Paradise Lost*, interfere with the interest. . . . Prometheus is, as it were, the type of the highest perfection of moral and intellectual nature, impelled by the purest and truest motives to the best and noblest ends.

That Shelley should have misinterpreted the character of Aeschylus's Prometheus is a small matter. The point is that Shelley isolates the character from the play, as he does Satan from *Paradise Lost*, and puts all the stress upon it in that isolation. The following passage from a school-edition of the play shows indirectly how the character-criterion has persisted:

> The structure of the play is not elaborate. A kind of plot is furnished by Prometheus' secret, but the thread is twice introduced and dropped again aimlessly, before being finally taken up to lead to the catastrophe. The episodes of Oceanus and Io each serve a dramatic object, but their introduction is naïvely abrupt. Oceanus interrupts the

narrative promised by Prometheus to the Chorus. Io's entry is quite casual and unexplained.

Such statements could only come from someone unaware that plot can have any powerful significance at all, someone who looks for a superficial regularity in plot and when he finds it looks no deeper; and that because he assumes that all the main significance must belong to character. Actually the play works primarily through plot, and the longest episode, that of Io, is the main instrument. Prometheus is a great static figure chained to the rock: Io, driven by the gadfly, cuts in her wanderings across the static figure. That is all, but it means everything. In character Prometheus and Io are richly and carefully contrasted. Prometheus is intensely conscious. He has complete knowledge of what he is doing, what the issues are, what he will suffer. He is also the inventor, the man who plans ahead, the pioneer. Io is ignorant of what her sufferings are all about. She is the helpless tool of the gods. The pattern of Io cutting across the perpendicular figure of the Titan expresses Aeschylus's sense of the great human paradox: the contrast of mankind conscious, provident, resourceful, and mankind hopelessly swayed by its own blind instincts. Far from Io's entry being casual, the Chorus, immediately before it, sing of the very qualities she embodies:

εἰπὲ ποῦ τίς ἀλκά;
τίς ἐφαμερίων ἄρηξις ; οὐδ' ἐδέρχθης
ὀλιγοδρανίαν ἄκικυν,
ἰσόνειρον, ᾇ τὸ φωτῶν
ἀλαὸν γένος ἐμπεποδισμένον.[1]

And Io's first words after she enters are a series of bewildered questions. To put the sole emphasis on character

---

[1] 'Tell me, what help is there, and where, in creatures of a day? What aid? Didst thou not behold the helpless infirmity, like a dream, in which the blind generation of men is shackled?'

is to distort Aeschylus's play, whose main meaning is one of the great commonplaces, stated through plot, obliquely.

The nineteenth century insisted on making Milton's Satan more important than the poem in which he occurred, with the result that the majestic sweep of the plot was left out of account. Satan may have grown to dimensions originally unintended by his creator, and may thereby somewhat impair the balance of the whole. But he in no wise breaks the vast progression of the poem. The action begins in Hell, is paralleled by the happenings in Heaven, narrows gradually to the universe, to earth seen from without, and reaches its climax on the narrow tragic stage of the Garden of Eden imagined from within. It comes to rest in a world enlarged to the measure of the world we know. In its sum this majesty of plot means more than Satan, and to put the main emphasis on him is to distort the poem.

But though in *Prometheus Bound* and *Paradise Lost* character is subordinate to plot, it is still a powerful means of oblique expression; and as long as it is recognised as subordinate there is no harm in considering it separately. Thus Io may be allowed to stand as the oblique expression of ideas on the blindly instinctive side of human nature, Satan of a certain conception of villainy.

To leave these two poems and to speak generally, it is when the portrayal of people emerges from the state of characterisation into that of character that direct gives way to oblique expression. There is much good characterisation in Crabbe; but his separate characters are little remembered, they have not begun to be proverbial. On the whole his poetry is direct: the poetry of observation and record. When a poet succeeds in making his persons memorable characters and not merely good examples of characterisation he will be found to be using them as the oblique expression of ideas. They will appear as types, the type implying an idea about kinds of people. If they are characters in this sense they may or may not be good examples of characterisation also. The Byronic hero is defective in this; he behaves rather ludicrously and is certainly not very true to average human behaviour. But his various embodiments, whether as Childe Harold or Manfred, do combine to create something we remember. They are the oblique (though wasteful and clumsy) expression of a general notion : that of banishment. Only, the Byronic hero is more complicated than the traditional figure of the exile, being divided not only from society but within himself. Chaucer's Wife of Bath, though an exaggerated character, differs from the Byronic hero in being a successful piece of characterisation : the poetry through which she is made known to us is, like Crabbe's, that of observation and record. But Chaucer also succeeds in expressing through her what can be called the Amazonian idea : she is a highly memorable character, a successful type.

Characters of the stature of the Wife of Bath are really embodiments of a great commonplace and they are created in the manner proper to obliquity. They do not translate a preconceived idea but are themselves the idea. To the greatest characters thus created we are apt to give an adjectival form—Falstaffian, Quixotic—thereby confessing that the author has embodied his ideas so effectively that his embodiment is more expressive than our own abstract and descriptive way of putting them.

If an excursion into prose may be allowed, Pickwick will serve to illustrate the last paragraph. No one could suppose that Dickens in his early years created this character on any abstract idea. Nor does Pickwick seem to be borrowed ready-made. His was a spontaneous birth. Yet, behaving consistently throughout his career, he reveals with extreme clarity the commonplaces of which he is the oblique expression. Full of curiosity and the zest for life he never misses an experience if he can help it; he always wants others to be happy; and he is innocent and credulous beyond anything possible in real life. In his first characteristic he embodies, airily and in the realm of light comedy, the idea of man the pioneer:

another version of which was Robinson Crusoe. In his second he preaches the doctrine of loving your neighbour as yourself. In his third, it would hardly be correct to say that he represents the child, for children are capable of learning by experience. Pickwick never learns, and he embodies an abstract idea of eternal childishness. Dickens achieves all this not by anything that has shape enough to be called plot, but by the gradual accumulation of incident. In the end he accumulated more incident than was needed, and the character of Pickwick is repeated rather than shown in process of growth. The evolution of Pickwick may thus go to prove that, in spite of Prometheus and Satan as interpreted above, a character may be the main obliquity in a book and dwarf the plot in importance; and that one should not allow recent predilections for plot-pattern to rule out that possibility. It may even happen that Hamlet will once again be thought more important than the play in which he occurs.

* * *

There are other means of obliquity than those discussed in this chapter. But samples enough have been given. To discuss more would upset the proportions of a short book. I now leave the topic of obliquity considered apart from statement and go on to discuss the relations of the two kinds of poetry.

Chapter IV

THE RELATIONS
OF DIRECT AND OBLIQUE

THIS chapter is historical. It consists of some notes on the changing status of direct and oblique poetry at certain epochs in literary history.

At the beginning of the European tradition the relations of direct and oblique poetry are simple and satisfactory. Homer has his obliquities but he can describe what for him were true happenings in the most direct manner. Hesiod can be straightforwardly didactic. The possibility of a large change came with the discovery in fifth century Greece of how to think more abstractly. Before the habit of abstract thought many ideas could be expressed only through the example, that is obliquely. There was no other choice. The way the poets used the gods is sufficient illustration. In Homer's day the gods had two reasons for existing: objective belief and their use for projecting purely human states of mind. They existed and they had to be propitiated; and Homer did not question that existence. He also uses them for the ends of poetic obliquity and for no more. When he tells how Zeus stirred up the Trojans to fight, it is his oblique way of saying that the Trojans stirred themselves up to fight. *The Odyssey* ends with the account of how Odysseus worked himself up or was worked up to take vengeance on the suitors of Penelope. Now it is Athena who constantly contrives Odysseus's acts and who prompts his state of mind. At times she does interpose with supernatural help; but mainly she serves to express obliquely Odysseus's own impulses. She tells him to disguise himself and go to find Eumaeus; but the whole action is so in keeping with Odysseus's own cautious and crafty nature that one cannot doubt that in some sense Odysseus thought of the plan himself. It would be unlike him to go to his palace in his own person. Homer, then, uses the gods for the oblique expression of psychological details.

In the Attic tragedians the gods have similar but more elaborate functions than in Homer. Euripides both uses the gods to clear up his plot with an ingenuousness surpassing Homer's and makes them something larger than the projection of ordinary human motives. Aphrodite in the *Hippolytus* in a way embodies Phaedra's instincts, but she also expresses obliquely ideas about those instincts. Euripides felt Phaedra's innocence and helplessness, and expressed them by transferring her motives from her own mind, where she would have had the responsibility for them, to the external force whither her responsibility could not extend. The result is the minimum of general statement.

Euripides stands on the threshold of the new order of things. I doubt whether at the date of the *Hippolytus* (428 B.C.) the idea of Phaedra's instincts could have been expressed otherwise than through a god, whether statement could cope with anything more complicated than unmixed volition. And if this is true, it will illustrate admirably how, for any of the subtler forms of experience, obliquity was the only form of expression: there was no other choice.

What has happened since Euripides's age is this. Where previously the poets simply had not the option of going wrong, they now had the temptation to try to be poets through the short cut of a borrowed method of abstract thought. When large ideas could only be put concretely, the smaller people had no means whatever of expressing them at all; when it was possible to formulate large ideas in the language of abstract argument, the smaller people could assimilate those ideas and translate them into verse. Ambitious, pretentious, and unscrupulous poets were thus given a chance of deceiving, such as had not existed before. And further, even among the reputable, there might be the temptation to choose a 'great' subject, a subject approved of by the intellect, and then to turn it into verse.

THE RELATIONS OF DIRECT AND OBLIQUE

One of the worst pieces of advice ever given was that of Arnold's, when, speaking of the highest poetical production, he said, 'Choose a fitting subject.' When the poet does that, he writes a *Merope*. The proper retort to the Arnoldian critic is to bid him heed the familiar example of the oyster. The pearl-making oyster does not choose the occasion of its pearl but is chosen by it. The poet's mind is a general mass of oysterdom. An alien grain of sand gets in, and the oysterdom seizes on it and grows round it till the pearl is formed and becomes autonomous. Till late in the fifth century B.C. *Meropes* could not exist; if poems were bad they were bad in other ways, they were weak or clumsy rather than spurious: afterwards the *Meropes*, and much worse the *Festuses* or the *Torchbearers*, could and did exist.

In the English Middle Ages the relations between direct and oblique poetry were healthy. Direct poetry suffered, when it did suffer, from its proper vice of dullness not from its improper vice of pretentiousness. And when it was good, as with Gower, it served to educate an audience into a fitness to appreciate something higher. Between Chaucer and the Elizabethans the two kinds of poetry keep their proper bounds, but the quality falls off. In particular, direct poetry is too poor to help the higher kind. Hawes could not have been much help to the best of Skelton and Wyatt. But in the early Elizabethan age the unpretentious moralising of *A Mirror for Magistrates* and of *Gorboduc*, expressed in forms that were new or experimental and that were very conscious of themselves, together with the mass of journeyman work in translating serves the typical functions of direct poetry very efficiently; preparing the way for the obliquities of Spenser.

In the full Elizabethan age most kinds co-exist including a great deal of embroidered statement. To the variety, good quality, and high utility of Elizabethan poetry of statement justice is not usually done. I mean such works as Daniel's *Civil Wars*, Drayton's *Barons' Wars* and *Heroical Epistles*, Sir John Davies's *Nosce Teipsum*, and much complimentary writing in the decasyllabic couplet. This verse was in high repute in its day; and though the general reader does not spend much time on it, he need not be unaware of its contemporary utility. Performing its function less neatly but more variedly and interestingly, it was doing for its age much what Gower did for his. Like the drama, though in a different way, it shows how unquestioned a part poetry had in people's lives during the age of Elizabeth. And it was this unquestionedness that helped to make Shakespeare and Milton possible. But not every Elizabethan poet admitted the poetry of statement. Donne, great as he is, reveals the penalty that must be paid for revolting too vehemently against worthy pedestrianism. It was well that he should turn against the Petrarchisers and develop the tougher lyric manner of Sidney and Raleigh and intensify in his satires the intellectualism of Marlowe and Chapman. But we should not, through admiration of *The Ecstasy* or the *Third Satire*, be blind to the penalty he incurred by cutting himself off from the cool argumentative excellence, the perfection of simple statement, found for instance in Daniel's *Ulysses and the Siren*. No dislike of Petrarchising justified ignoring the model of lines like these:

> Fair nymph, if fame and honour were
>   To be attained with ease,
> Then would I come and rest me there,
>   And leave such toils as these.
> But here it dwells, and here must I
>   With danger seek it forth:
> To spend the time luxuriously
>   Becomes not men of worth.

It was through its failure to command this kind of writing as well as others that the Metaphysical school tempted the Augustan age to react too far and to put on the poetry of statement a value which it could not bear. Milton, mindful of the fine balance of Ben Jonson, made no such error.

For all his individualism he knew his duty to society, and he expresses it in his verse. In his *Epitaph on the Marchioness of Winchester* he yields gracefully to the best-bred conventions of his age; and his next essays in this metre, *L'Allegro* and *Il Penseroso*, written while he was still at Cambridge, show their kinship to the poetry of simple statement by their elegant social tone. Had it not been for such a kinship, it is not at all certain that Milton could have evolved a style that was tolerable in a long poem.

For giving a new turn to the relations between direct and oblique poetry Dryden is important. Though a great enough poet to command certain large obliquities, he did more than anyone else to weight direct as against oblique poetry, finally displacing the Elizabethan balance. He found the poetry of statement in not too good a way. Davenant and Chamberlayne are weak and indeterminate compared with Daniel and Drayton. Cowley, who should have been the Gower of his age, affected the style of Donne, which rarely became him well. The competent and lucid drama of Massinger and Shirley had been killed by the closing of the theatres. No wonder if the thin but competent elegance of Waller and Denham gave to Dryden the promise of better things. Anyhow, though Dryden did much else, he did in *Religio Laici* and *The Hind and the Panther* raise the level of the poetry of statement to a technical height it had not reached before, thus quite altering its status. And even if *Religio Laici* has an oblique meaning, it was not this that was to be so influential in shaping Augustan poetry.

Pope, though gifted with a kind of sensibility that required oblique expression, was not powerful enough to modify the tradition derived from Dryden for anyone but himself. He was indeed able to express himself through the nominally direct and social, but he did not succeed in persuading his age that direct and social verse was not the best verse. There is much good direct verse in the eighteenth century, but it was unsupplemented by the oblique kind. And no amount of admiration for Thomson or Goldsmith or Crabbe can excuse an age for its failure to listen to Blake. However, the eighteenth century tradition did not go stale till the Victorian age, and, more than most of them knew, the great Romantic poets rose to their eminence from the assurance given by the solid tradition of the previous age. To be familiar with *The Seasons* was to be prepared to appreciate *Tintern Abbey*, and the good sense of Augustan didactic verse is the necessary point of departure for the greater richness and allusiveness of *Don Juan*.

As a basis on which to erect sublimer poetry, the poetry of statement is not valid for an indefinite time; and the nineteenth century in general made the mistake of not replacing the eighteenth century type with one of its own. Instead, it degraded the status of direct poetry altogether. There are some notable exceptions; but as a rule the nineteenth century either transformed the poetry of statement by an unseemly inflation, or robbed it of all seriousness. Typical of the first error is a poem like Bailey's *Festus*. It is devoid of obliquity, and it strains the old statement-technique to include the great passions and the eternal verities.

> Men who walk up to fame as to a friend,
> Or their own house, which from the wrongful heir
> They have wrested, from the world's hard hand and gripe,
> Men who, like death, all bone and all unarm'd,
> Have taken the giant world by the throat and thrown him,
> And made him swear to maintain their name and fame
> At peril of his life; who shed great thoughts
> As easily as an oak looseneth its golden leaves
> In a kindly largesse to the soil it grew on;
> Whose names are ever on the world's broad tongue,
> Like sound upon the falling of a force;
> Whose words, if winged, are with angels' wings;
> Who . . . etc., etc.

This is what ousted the soberer passions and solider prosody of a poem like Young's *Night Thoughts*.

By the time Tennyson began to write, the poetical state of affairs was the opposite of what it had been in the eighteenth century. Then it had been solid below but incomplete above; now an imposing superstructure was to be erected on a defective base. What is so noticeable about the Victorian poets is how little help they give one another; how greatly the general social nexus of versifying has been loosened. There are isolated groups, but no common stock of poetising, taken for granted. Even the bond of hate has loosened. How many of the poetical maladies of the age are due to the degeneration of statement it is difficult to say, but I cannot doubt its great influence. Tennyson is a victim of it. With a strange, rare, but self-distrustful nature he stood in need of a solid social basis of poetry. Something taken for granted would have helped his uncertain spirit. It would also have given him some sort of standard of style in the less personal of his longer poems. But by rejecting Byron in favour of Keats instead of allowing room for them both, or in other words by renouncing the great tradition of statement poetry with its strong social trend, Tennyson signed his own death-warrant as a writer of the larger poetical forms. For, when he writes at length, he flags.

With Browning the case is different. He did write a good deal of social verse; and it is what he was best fitted for. Where a tradition of statement would have helped was to assure him that such verse was very much worth while and to encourage him to take greater pains with it. Had the Augustan tradition survived, Browning might have done work of high importance in adapting the old general treatment of human nature to particular human beings. He could have carried on that widening of sympathy referred to in *Don Juan*.

The relations or lack of relations between Tennyson and Browning illustrate the melancholy truth of how little one poet helped another in the nineteenth century from the Victorian period on. *Men and Women* appeared in 1855, the first of *Idylls of the King* in 1859. The two

works have no contact. Any promise of healthy directness that was contained in *Up at a Villa* and kindred poems
was cut off by the *Idylls* and their great popularity. The
Idylls captured a wide public to whom an unassuming and
healthy directness might have appealed. They temporarily killed social verse and encouraged the bad easi-
ness of the day-dream at the expense of an easy but sound
poetry of statement. This is not to condemn the tradition
of sensuous, unrealistic, pictorial verse that runs from
Keats through the early Tennyson to the Pre-Raphaelite
poets, but that such verse should have become so dominant
was not right.

There are signs to-day of a wish to revive direct poetry,
and it is worth asking whether there is any lead such a
revival could follow. The eighteenth century tradition
(which is now the most favoured) is so distant and the
break with it was so serious that it cannot be restored. It
is more profitable to remember that direct poetry did not
die out in the nineteenth century, even if it was not very
effective. Indeed, about the middle of the century the
case of direct poetry looked more hopeful. There was
Arnold who though he never made his verse social was
a craftsman and could argue clearly and elegantly. He
did stand for some of the virtues of direct statement.
Clough's *Amours de Voyage* is poetry of statement with
virtues and vices just the opposite of Arnold's. It is
loosely wrought compared with Arnold's best but has an
agreeable social tone passing from play to earnest with an
ease Arnold could never achieve. About the same time
Patmore began publishing *The Angel in the House*. Whatever his poetical achievement here, at least he deserves
praise in having tried to strike a balance between the
direct and the oblique in poetry. And he deserves a
longer note in this context than his relative poetical
merit would seem to warrant.

Patmore may or may not have been successful in expressing an erotic mysticism through a mild modern love-
story, but at least he made a courageous experiment. And

that experiment included the typical virtues of the poetry of statement as well as certain others. Patmore's reputation has suffered through readers not understanding the nature of his banalities. This passage from *The Angel in the House* has caused a good deal of merriment:

> I laugh'd and sigh'd; for I confess
>   I never went to Ball, or Fête,
> Or Show, but in pursuit express
>   Of my predestinated mate;
> And thus to me, who had in sight
>   The happy chance upon the cards,
> Each beauty blossom'd in the light
>   Of tender personal regards;
>
> And, in the records of my breast,
>   Red-letter'd, eminently fair,
> Stood sixteen, who, beyond the rest,
>   By turns till then had been my care
> At Berlin three, one at St. Cloud,
>   At Chatteris, near Cambridge, one,
> At Ely four, in London two,
>   Two at Bowness, in Paris none,
> And, last and best, in Sarum three.

To laugh at this is to misunderstand Patmore, to imagine that he meant to be poetical and failed; whereas his elegantly lowered tone makes it plain that he knows what he is doing and has no pretensions to any dignity beyond what the mere fact of versifying imposes. Patmore seeks the miraculous in the quotidian, and his method is to show the quotidian unheightened, that any sublimity which springs from it may exhibit the more authentic an exaltation. In fact there is little to object to in Patmore's lines except that they run the risk of tedium if long protracted; and they have some solid virtues. They are well wrought, with clever emphasis and variations of tempo; there is no straining after effect. And these variations suggest a flexibility that will easily allow the verse-form to take on greater seriousness. The passage then is capable of being both a norm of contrast for more heightened poetry and of suggesting that this more heightened poetry could be forthcoming. And it is an achievement to rise from the lowliness of the passage quoted to such a piece of writing as this:

> Right art thou who would'st rather be
> A doorkeeper in Love's fair house,
> Than lead the wretched revelry
> Where fools at swinish troughs carouse.
> But do not boast of being least;
> And if to kiss thy Mistress' skirt
> Amaze thy brain, scorn not the Priest
> Whom greater honours do not hurt,
> Stand off and gaze, if more than this
> Be more than thou canst understand,
> Revering him whose power of bliss,
> Angelic, dares to seize her hand,
> Or whose seraphic love makes flight
> To the apprehension of her lips;
> And think, the sun of such delight
> From thine own darkness takes eclipse.
> And, wouldst thou to the same aspire,
> This is the art thou must employ,
> Live greatly; so shalt thou acquire
> Unknown capacities of joy.

My last example from about this period, Mrs. Browning's *Aurora Leigh* (1857), has perhaps fewer of the typical qualities of the poetry of statement. It has not the virtue of consistently good workmanship; in fact the verse is only good when the authoress happens to be particularly interested in what she is saying. And the less emotional passages form a poor background for the more emotional. But it has the virtue of being social, of being permeated with the sense of living human beings; and at its best it can delight us with the enthusiastic way in which it describes the human passions.

But all these examples were too miscellaneous to create a tradition, and direct poetry has remained fitful ever since. And nearer or in our own day Kipling, Masefield, and Miss Sackville-West, though they have done well to reach a large public through direct verse, have neither belonged to nor created any strong tradition.

If there has been a decline in the quality and status of direct poetry since the eighteenth century, it may be asked whether the process should not be carried further still: to a point where it exists only as supplying a minimum of intelligibility to a higher kind, not in its own right at all. The argument for this might run as follows.

To pretend that to-day things are as they were when Thomson's *Seasons* went into edition after edition and was really read in most cultured homes, is useless. Even in the last century the reading of easy poetry formed a far bigger part of life than it does to-day. In the middle Victorian age many fathers were in the habit of reading aloud to their families the later poems of Tennyson as they were published. It is plain enough that now things are different. The kind of attention that went to the easier forms of verse goes to popular science or philosophy. The poetry of statement has been crowded out; and it is hopeless to revive an anachronism. Not only is the poetry of statement dead, but there are several reasons why it ought to be. Only the concentrated and strenuous activities can be allowed in a strenuous age. When there is so much to be done and experienced, anything suspected of being a time-waster must go. Travelling by air you must cut down your luggage. There may be room for an omnibus-volume of hundred-per-cent. masterpieces, but Gower and all he stands for are junk. That is what the world might say: the critics might come to the same goal by a different road. In recent years the range of knowledge exacted from the literary critic is far higher than it was. In the eighteenth century it was no disgrace not to have read Dante, Villon, or Donne; and the great foreign novelists had not yet appeared. To-day, when a critic thinks he should be familiar with the masterpieces of four or five literatures, how can he have time to meditate on the poetry of statement in his own tongue? How can he be in the mood for *The Seasons* when his conscience is telling him that Leopardi is still unread and that his knowledge of *Bouvard et Pécuchet* rests on hearsay alone? And for the mind crowded with masterpieces detective fiction is a more suitable relaxation than second-grade verse. Reinforcing this conscientious focusing on masterpieces is the still-potent nineteenth century theory that only pure poetry is to be tolerated. The old long poem was a series of lyrics artificially joined by pieces of versified prose; and only the lyrics had value. With this knowledge we should write lyrics alone: nothing else is poetry. To Symbolist theory, statement-poetry is a contradiction of terms; for the health of poetry statement must be relegated to prose.

What can be said on the other side?

First, as was pointed out through the examples of Kipling, Masefield, and Miss Sackville-West, it is not true that the poetry of statement is entirely dead, or that there is in fact no demand for it.

Secondly, for the question whether the poetry of statement ought to be dead. If mankind could reduce his poetical luggage to the omnibus-volume of hundred-per-cent. masterpieces and could both enjoy the volume and continue to add to it, the argument for scrapping statement-poetry would be strong. But masterpieces do not get their full effect in isolation; and the only background that suits them is one of good but less intense poetry. Many people to-day think that the novel makes as good a background. This is an illusion. To appreciate great verse, you must have the experience of much verse-reading. Prose is no substitute. And to get the feel of the actual verse, nothing serves so well as good statement-poetry. Lamentable as it may be that matters of an apparently intenser interest have to be sacrificed to reading second-grade verse, without that sacrifice the final poetic reward cannot be attained. Nor can obliquity itself be healthy unless founded on a living poetry of statement. Novel-writing, for instance, is no substitute as a basis. D. H. Lawrence is an apt illustration. In comparison with the man's genius his verse is ineffective; and largely because wrongly based. It has little to do with verse in general, but is a parasite on the tree of an ecstatic prose. This does not preclude the doubt whether prose has not usurped successfully the main territory not only of direct but of oblique poetry. Though you cannot derive great verse from great prose, you might derive from sound prose a great prose that has the attributes of the greatest verse. Thus some might consider the best of Hardy's novels to fulfil the functions of great poetry better than any contemporary verse, and *To the Lighthouse* or *The Waves* to be more truly poetical than *The Waste Land*. This is a tenable position, though I do not hold it, and I prefer it to the heresy that something other than good verse can be the foundation of the greatest verse. But, granted that verse will continue to have a function, for its proper health it must strive to recapture *all* the qualities proper to the poetry of statement.

How this is to come about is at the moment quite obscure; but this obscurity does not make the necessity any more avoidable. Nor is it wise to despair of a revival of direct poetry, any more than to acquiesce in the common opinion that the epic is dead for good and all. Thirty years ago the case of the verse drama seemed quite as hopeless, and yet that form has come to life again. If mankind decides it wants poetry at all, and if direct poetry is needed as the background of oblique, then surely, even if after a long period of trial and error, it will be practised in its plenitude once again.

Chapter V

EPILOGUE

THE sentiments expressed in the last chapter are controversial. I hope they will not prejudice the reader against the rest of the book; for my main intention is separate from any moral concerning the relations of the two kinds of poetry. It has indeed more to do with practical than with theoretical criticism. Though it may be worth while distinguishing between direct and oblique statement, indicating the transition from the one kind to the other, and discussing various means of obliquity, I am interested above all in guessing at the feelings, experiences, or ideas that underlie the apparent subject-matter of oblique poetry, for this is a type of criticism of which, if it is of any value, there might be more. The final question to be met is, has it any value?

There are two ways in which the interpretation of obliquity may turn out to be valueless. Either it may lead to such hopeless divergences of opinion that it proves to be nothing more than the exercise of individual caprice, or, granted sufficient congruity of opinion, it may not in fact heighten most people's appreciation of poetry.

The first danger can be assessed by experiment alone. When a sufficient number of intelligent readers test a sufficient number of oblique poems by their own responses we shall know whether the game is worth playing or not. I think that success is possible with some poems read by the right persons in the right mood. In other words, illumination is largely a matter of luck. The sceptical will find their doubts expressed by Aldous Huxley in his essay *Music at Night*. He believes that the limits of this kind of criticism are quickly reached. Yet even if they are (and I think he exaggerates), his demonstrations of what is behind a Madonna of Piero della Francesca and one of Tura argue that you can get far enough at least to be interesting. And helpful? But that brings me to the second possible danger.

Supposing I am right in seeing in *Lycidas* an oblique statement of the commonplace that personal integrity is what ultimately matters, have I done anything to help readers to enjoy the poem? Certainly at first sight it would seem arrogant and brutally tactless to insist on telling what the poet has had the instinct or the intention not to tell. When a large part of the poem's virtue consisted in the actual silence, is it not desecration to disturb it? I would answer: It all depends on the reader. Those readers who are poets themselves and who have read a particular poem as poets will gain little from the conscious explaining of obliquity. They will read the poem as the poet conceived it: they will apprehend the idea in the instance and will have no use for the abstracted idea. But then there are very few such readers. What about the rest? Is it not better for the common reader to have obliquity laboriously translated that he may grasp it than to miss it altogether? For the practice of criticism in the past has made it plain how much obliquity has actually been undetected, with what cheerfully callous straight-forwardness the poet's profundities have been passed over. Nor does the common defence of all analytical criticism fail the type with which I have been concerned: namely, that in the readings which succeed analysis the conscious effort of splitting up can be succeeded by a now juster fitting together. If De Quincey's little essay has helped us to analyse the Porter's soliloquy in *Macbeth*, we do not in re-reading the play necessarily have any conscious recollection of the criticism. Our response will have been modified, but De Quincey has not usurped the place of Shakespeare.

My own experience is that detection of obliquity has helped appreciation. Blake's *Echoing Green* has become at once simpler and profounder since I have seen an idea behind it. What had puzzled me is now plain; and what

EPILOGUE

I had enjoyed in it is the more enjoyable as a part of a greater harmony. And I believe the common reader agrees: at least in principle, if not with this particular instance. Nor can the poets afford to neglect the common reader: for they depend on him for the encouragement to write as well as they can. And this being so, even they may admit that a second-best method of apprehending poetry may have its uses.

So believing, I have written this book.

INDEX

114

INDEX

INDEX

Printed in Great Britain
by T. and A. CONSTABLE LTD., Hopetoun Street
Printers to the University of Edinburgh